THE WORLD OF
THE TRAPP FAMILY

Text by William Anderson
Photography by David Wade

Anderson, William
The World of The Trapp Family

Published by:
Anderson Publications

Visit the author on the web at:
www.williamandersonbooks.com

ISBN #1-890757-00-4
Printed in Hong Kong

Book Design, Production & Jacket Design
Terry Bickmore, White Raven Design
Santa Barbara, CA

Edited by:
Cynthia Anderson
Julie Simpson

Distributed by:
The Trapp Family Lodge
Stowe, VT 05672
Tel: 1-800-826-7000

Visit the Trapp Family on the web at:
www.trappfamily.com

This book is dedicated to the Trapp Family,
past and present. With their sense of mission,
their music, their faith and their courage,
they have inspired the world.

"I know your deeds,
your love and faith,
your service and perseverance..."

Revelations 2:9

THE TRAPP FAMILY

Rupert
1911 - 1992

Married in 1947 to
Henriette Lajoie

Married (second)
to Janice Tyre

George
Monique
Elizabeth
Christopher
Stephanie
Françoise

Agathe
1913 -

Maria
1914 -

Werner
1915 -

Married in 1948 to
Erika Klambauer

Barbara
Martin
Bernhard
Elisabeth
Tobias
Stephan

Hedwig
1917 - 1972

Agathe Whitehead von Trapp
1890 - 1922
Married 1911

Georg Ritter von Trapp
1880 - 1947

Maria Augusta Kutschera von Trapp
1905 - 1987
Married 1927

Johanna
1919 - 1994

Martina
1921 - 1951

Rosmarie
1929 -

Eleonore
1931 -

Johannes Georg
1939 -

Married in 1948 to
Ernst Florian Winter

Married in 1949 to
Jean Dupire

Married in 1954 to
Hugh D. Campbell

Married in 1969 to
Lynne Peterson

Ernst (desceased)
Johanna
Florian
Notburga
Agathe
Hemma
Severin

Notburga (deceased)

Elizabeth
Peggy
Jeanie
Polly
Erika
Hope
Martina

Kristina
Sam

Table of Contents

Acknowledgements

The concept for this book originated in Japan with Yumiko Taniguchi, and a version was published in 1995 by Ryutaro Adachi of the Kyuryudo Art Book Publishing Company of Tokyo. The enthusiastic acceptance of the book in Japan attests to the universal quality of the Trapp Family story, and this led to the belief that an American edition was needed.

The Trapp Family's willingness to share their lives again in book form made this volume possible. Each, in his or her own individual way, contributed to this comprehensive documentary. Input from the following members of the original Trapp Family Singers is greatly appreciated: Agathe von Trapp, Maria von Trapp, Rosmarie von Trapp, Eleonore von Trapp Campbell, Werner von Trapp, and Johannes von Trapp.

Earlier contributions of the following persons, no longer here to see this book, are equally valued: Baroness Maria von Trapp, Rupert von Trapp, Johanna von Trapp Winter, and Monsignor Franz Wasner. It was Rupert who wrote, "Your plan for a factual, historical account of the Trapp Family and the cultural treasure we were privileged to bring here is not only interesting, but to me, very important."

Other family members assisted in ways small and large. They include George von Trapp, Elisabeth von Trapp Hall, Hemma Rusoff, Notburga von Trapp, and Ernst F. Winter.

During the compilation of the book, the staff at the Trapp Family Lodge was very helpful, as well as Stefan Herzl of Salzburg Panorama Tours. Harold Peterson, Barbara Stechow Harris, and Annette Brophy Jacobs, former members of the Trapp Family Singers, offered their memories and photographs. Ruth Murdoch, another family friend, shared her recollections.

All historical photography, unless otherwise credited, is used through the courtesy of the Trapp Family. Most of these photographs were taken during the 1940s and 1950s by Herbert Matter and Robert M. Lewis, under the direction of Alix Williamson, who for twenty-five years ably served as the Trapp Family Singers' publicist and press representative. She was responsible for the design, copy and layout of promotional materials in this book which advertised the Trapps' concerts and music camp.

The job of layout and design for a book with so many images is a formidable task; we are deeply indebted to Bill Stanhope of Pembroke, Massachusetts for his help and expertise in the initial design.

Our very special thanks go to designer Terry Bickmore for her patient and valiant efforts to cope with and coordinate collaborators Anderson in Michigan and Wade in Maine and Japan. From her design studio in California faxes flew back and forth, phone calls reached monumental proportions as we all searched for the perfect way to crystallize this far-reaching story of the Trapp Family, in a truly international endeavor. In the same way that Maria von Trapp kept to a rigorous concert schedule until her last child was born, Terry labored to design and bring to life this book until just a few hours before the birth of her second child, Cooper. Every page here is a tribute to her talent and endurance; her dedication is greatly appreciated.

A sincere thanks to all.
W.T.A.

Chapter 1

The von Trapps of Austria

Austria is one of the world's most beautiful countries. The Alps stretch their peaks heavenward across the country, with green valleys, pristine lakes, and dense forests between the mountains. Quiet farms dot the glens, with snow-capped mountain ranges as a backdrop.

The Austrians love their land, but they also love their culture. On the Danube River, the capital city of Vienna has always been a haven for artists, musicians, writers, and thinkers. Music has constantly enlivened the Austrians, and their musicians have given the world some of its most memorable melodies from the pens of Schubert, Haydn, Brahms, Strauss, and Mozart.

Most of the country is Roman Catholic, and the festivals, pageantry, and music connected with the church have always been important traditions within the lives of Austrian families. It is this mixture of faith, celebration, and music-making that helped to create Austria's most famous and beloved musical family, the von Trapps.

The saga of the Trapp Family had its origins during the days of the Austro-Hungarian Empire. The Austrian Empire, combined with the Kingdom of Hungary, was ruled by the Hapsburgs. The empire consisted of several different nationalities and languages, each retaining its own customs. The land mass included both the towering Alps and the seacoast on the Adriatic.

Soon after the formation of the Austro-Hungarian Empire in 1867, August Johann Trapp joined the Austrian Navy. While commanding the SMS *Saida* in the Mediterranean, August Trapp saw his ship safely through a ferocious storm. His bravery and tactical maneuvers came to the attention of Emperor Franz Joseph, who bestowed knighthood upon August von Trapp in 1876. The *von*, added to his name after knighthood, and the title were hereditary, passing on to his children.

There were three children born to August von Trapp and his wife Hedwig. The oldest son, Georg, was born on April 4, 1880 at Zara, then the capital of Dalmatia and an Austrian port. The Navy was in the boy's blood, and at the age of fourteen he entered the Naval Academy at Fiume. "He was a bit of a rascal," his daughter Eleonore said of her father's student days. "But he was not one to shirk work, was fair to everyone, and much loved by his comrades."

Georg distinguished himself in technical and maritime studies, and in 1898 he joined his class on a lengthy voyage. Serving as a midshipman, he sailed to East Africa, Australia, and the Holy Land. He was so impressed with the South Seas that he always longed to return. The lure

Captain Georg von Trapp and his wife Agathe.

Facing page: The Austrian Alps were a background to the life of the Trapp Family. The seven children of the Captain and Agathe: Back Row: Rupert, Maria, and Agathe. Front Row: Johanna, Martina, Hedwig, and Werner.

The canniness of Captain von Trapp as a submarine commander is shown in this anecdote:

"One day, at the height of the unrestricted submarine warfare of World War I, on active duty in the combat area, I picked up a British destroyer following me. We zigzagged, maneuvered, did all the tricks known to sailors for throwing off pursuers. Still, that dogged, persistent, infernal destroyer kept on our trail. After four hours we were getting desperate, for if we didn't come up for air soon, we'd die of suffocation. At last I gave the order to come up. I got ready a barrel of oil. When we arose, I had the oil dumped just after we reached top. We took in air, quickly submerged. And, when we were in a position to observe again, the destroyer was steaming off, convinced, of course, that our last emergence was the last throes of the dying ship. Well, when I was again a position to observe, I noticed that one of my oil valves was leaking enough to send up to the surface a perfect trail which led that destroyer after us through those terrific four hours' chase."

Captain von Trapp was a highly decorated Navy hero of the old Austro-Hungarian empire.

of the sea was ever with him.

In 1900, when the Boxer Rebellion broke out in China, Austria sent ships to protect any countrymen who were endangered through the uprising. With a contingent of thirty other sailors, Georg von Trapp was involved in an Allied expedition which took the fort of Peitang. While there he encountered his first American troops, and developed a respect and admiration for them. Georg was decorated for gallantry and achieved the rank of captain in the Austrian Navy.

His rise in the Navy was a swift one; he was transferred from cruisers to battleships, and then to torpedo and destroyer flotillas. In 1908, he was licensed as an aviator.

Captain von Trapp was one of the first to envision the importance of submarine navigation. He applied for transfer to Fiume, where the newly invented torpedoes were being manufactured. There in

1909, after a society ball, he noticed a young woman playing the violin. Her gentle spirit and beauty immediately appealed to him, and he thought, "This is going to be my wife."

The sweet young woman was nineteen-year-old Agathe Whitehead, whose grandfather had invented the torpedo. At first her family discouraged a romance with the dark-eyed, mustachioed Captain von Trapp, but before long they were engaged. In January 1911, the young couple were married.

The first home of Georg and Agathe was at Pola, the seat of the Austrian Navy, overlooking the blue Adriatic. There their first child was born, a son named Rupert, in November 1911. Their second child, a daughter named Agathe, was born in March 1913. Those were happy times of peace for the family. Agathe was a capable young wife and mother, with a gentle sense of humor and a quiet understanding of her husband and his career. Together they created a secure, loving environment for their first two children.

World events shook the cozy security of the Trapp family in June 1914. Archduke Franz Ferdinand, on a visit to Sarajevo, was assassinated by a Serbian nationalist who favored self-rule from Austria. War on Serbia was declared by Austria-Hungary; countries took sides and World War I escalated.

Captain von Trapp was placed in charge of two of Austria's six primitive submarines,

Agathe and Georg von Trapp.

first U-5 and then U-14. Under great difficulties he commanded his crews, performing incredible feats. The Captain was a rare commander, making a team of his crew, who were of varied ethnic backgrounds, supporting his men and encouraging them.

Early in the war, all civilians were ordered to leave Pola, so

Above: Captain Georg von Trapp and navy friend, Erwin Wallner.

Left: Georg von Trapp was renowned for his humane approach in dealing with his crews.

Agathe packed up her children and went to the refuge of her mother's home in the Pinzgau region of Austria, at Zell-am-See. It was a difficult move, knowing that her husband was in danger and that it was uncertain when she could return to Pola, but Agathe approached every challenge calmly. Her mother was a widow and glad to have her family near. It was for this reason that she designed and built the picturesque country home on the lake shore called "Erlhof."

Grandmother Whitehead, whom the little von Trapps called "Gromi," was a dignified matriarch who managed her home with ease and provided a sense of wellbeing, despite the tragedies of war. Her daughters Agathe, Mary, and Joan knitted for soldiers on the front, played games with the children, sang, and made music to help pass the time. Although Georg came home for furloughs, he was not present when his third child, Maria, was born in 1914. A year later a son was born and named Werner, for his uncle who died during the war.

Daughter Agathe recalled the loving, secure quality of their upbringing and the role of their mother, whom the children called "Mama" —with the accent on the second syllable. "Mama loved her children and her own family. Her youngest sister, our Tante Joan, told me that Mama actually brought her up and told her useful things for her life . . . She knitted snowsuits for us all, as well as woolen caps and mittens. She

loved to sew and was very good at it. She made clothes for us, and I remember particularly our sailor suits and a bluish gray coat for me. I can still see Mama, Tante Mary, and Tante Connie (the widow of Georg's brother Werner) cutting material on the big dining room table. When I was a little older, Mama taught me how to knit and to make very small hemstitches . . . When we were sick, and we had all the early childhood diseases, she would care for us personally, taking turns with our nanny."

Zell-am-See was a haven of peace and natural beauty, seemingly tucked away from the horrors of the war. Life there revolved on a regular wheel of housekeeping, family visits, attending Mass, and romping through the countryside. To attend church or shop in town, a short boat ride across the lake from Erlhof was necessary. "Living on the other side of the lake, we were isolated," Maria remembered, "so we had to become self-sufficient with our own company."

One of the earliest experiences the von Trapp children remembered of the Erlhof days was family music-making. Their mother played piano and violin and sang folk songs with her sisters. Gromi played piano, too, sometimes "four-hands" style with her son Frank.

Captain von Trapp's brief respites at home were times to

The Trapp home in Pola, birthplace of Rupert and Agathe. The Kitzsteinhorn at Zell-am-See, which Maria von Trapp dubbed "The Pearl of Austria."

Top: Grandmother Whitehead's Erlhof at Zell-am-See Lake, which was the early home of the Trapp children. Above: Zell-am-See Lake.

relax from his grueling life in naval service and to become acquainted with his growing family. But all too soon, he was called back to the dismal business of war. His greatest feat for his country occurred in April 1915, when his submarine made an underwater launch at the French battleship *Leon Gambetta*. With a full moon rising eerily over the sea, the Captain and his crew risked their lives to sink the enemy ship and its crew of 600. He later described the battle as "a kind of a duel." Patriot though he was, Captain von Trapp always downplayed his significant leadership role and regretted the loss of life that transpired.

The sinking of the French ship fueled the enemy's fear of what was perceived as great Austrian force in undersea navigation. The Mediterranean became an area to avoid. Captain von Trapp was a national hero, his name a household word and a headline in the newspapers. He was given command of a captured French submarine, the *Curie*, which had been caught in a net in Pola. With this new craft he went on to sink over 60,000 tons of enemy shipping.

Georg and Agathe with their first five children: (from left) Agathe, Hedwig, Werner, Maria, and Rupert.

For his services, Captain von Trapp was recognized as one of the greatest heroes of the Imperial Navy. He was awarded the highest national honor, the Maria Theresian Cross, with the rights and privileges and title of "Baron." The new Baron von Trapp took his honor modestly; his daughter Eleonore observed, "He was always self-effacing, more concerned about others than himself."

Life at Erlhof continued at its slow, idyllic pace, almost as if there were no war waging. In July 1917, Georg and Agathe's third daughter was born and named Hedwig, after her paternal grandmother. That same year, 1917, America entered the war, bringing new manpower to the struggles. The Allies—Britain, France and Italy—formed the Supreme War Council to plan strategy. A year later, the war was over. On November 11, 1918, the armistice was signed. That same month, the last Hapsburg emperor was deposed, making Austria a republic.

For Agathe and the five von Trapp children, war's end meant the return of Papa, their husband and father. For Captain Georg von Trapp, it was the end of an era. The Navy was his calling, and he did his job in an outstanding manner. The Versailles Treaty stripped Austria of its seacoast; there was no more Austrian Navy. Georg described his feelings as this chap-

Captain von Trapp.

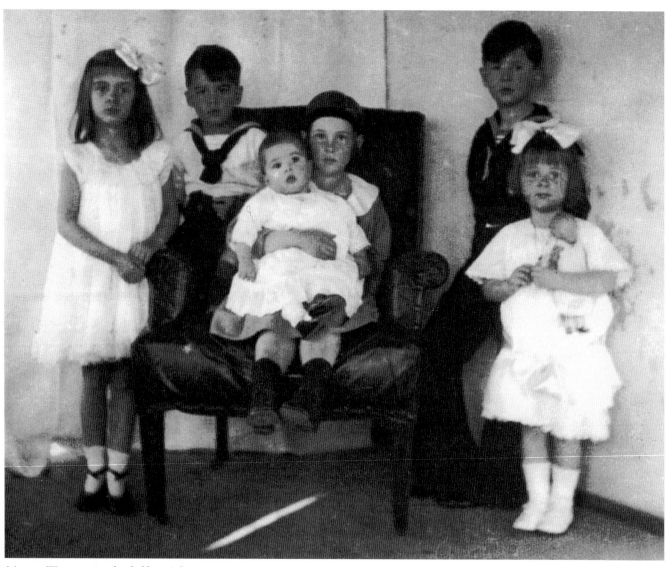

Maria, Werner, Agathe holding Johanna, Rupert, and Hedwig.

ter of his life closed in the book of memoirs he wrote later, *Bis Zum Letzten Flaggenschuss (To the Last Flag Salute)*.

When Captain von Trapp came home to his family, he was war-weary and faced with the problem of finding a permanent home for his wife and children. His chosen career over, he wholeheartedly assumed the position of head of the family. The rest of his life was spent as a kindly, understanding patriarch.

For awhile, the reunited

family remained at Erlhof and then lived nearby at a lake hotel called "Kitzsteinhorn." It was during this time, in 1919 that the fourth daughter, Johanna, was born. But despite the happiness a new baby's birth brings, Georg and Agathe were beset with the problems of providing a home for their large family. Kitzsteinhorn flooded, making it unlivable. Austria also was plagued by post-war shortages which affected all levels of society.

Agathe's brother Robert

offered a solution to the housing dilemma: he suggested that the von Trapps live in a house he owned at Klosterneuburg, near Vienna. The property had been the summer home of Austria's beloved empress, Maria Theresia, and was known as "Martinschlossel." The family settled into their new home early in 1921. Not long after, Georg and Agathe's seventh and last child was born and named Martina. It seemed appropriate; her birthplace stood on the Martinstrassee, close to the Martinkirche (church). The family was then complete: Rupert, Agathe, Maria, Werner, Hedwig, Johanna, and baby Martina.

Caring for the large family, the big house, and the broad surrounding grounds was accomplished by a staff of maids, a cook, a governess, and a nurse. Franz Stiegler, Georg's orderly from Navy days, also lived on the property with his family. He was a devoted friend of the Captain, and he cared for the animals, while Gustl, the gardener, oversaw the gardens and orchards so essential to feed the large household. With postwar shortages, most Austrians cultivated every available bit of soil.

Agathe von Trapp presided over the household of diverse people, ages, and needs. She even invited the Captain's widowed Irish sister-in-law and her daughter to join them. Daughter Agathe recalled that her mother "was beloved by all our servants, and those that survived the second World War remembered her with great affection, saying the best

time of their lives was when they were in our service."

The good times at Klosterneuburg did not last long, however. Scarlet fever invaded the von Trapp nursery, as an epidemic raged all over Klosterneuburg. The children had cases of varying severity, and finally Agathe contracted the disease.

For weeks, the thirty-two-year-old mother fought to recover. She was treated in a Vienna sanitarium for the after-effects of the illness. But her health did not return. On September 2, 1922, the bell in the Martinkirche sounded its solemn toll for Agathe von Trapp. She was buried in the graveyard outside Klosterneuburg, leaving behind her loving husband and family of seven children who were destined to travel far in the world as the Trapp Family Singers.

The grave of Agathe von Trapp.

Agathe von Trapp and her children, circa 1920.

19

CHAPTER 2

A Teacher for the von Trapps

Before Agathe von Trapp's death, she asked her husband to remarry. She sensed that their children, who were accustomed to tender nurturing, would need another motherly influence. At the time of their mother's death, Rupert was nearly eleven; Agathe was nine; Maria was eight; Werner was seven; Hedwig was five; Johanna was three; and Martina was one and a half.

Though the children were motherless, they lived in a web of security. Their governess, Fraulein Freckman, kept the days well-ordered with lessons, playtime, walks, meals, studying, and regular bedtime. By nature the children were cooperative and self-sufficient; they thrived on routine. Their schoolwork revealed signs of creative talent, and music lessons for the von Trapp children were pleasurable, not tedious.

Watching lovingly over the lives of his children was Captain von Trapp. Though he briefly participated in a shipping trade business in the North Sea and along the Danube, he spent most of the time close to the children. To further forge his role as father, the Captain converted from his parents' Lutheran faith to his childrens' Catholicism. "We really had a beautiful life," his daughter Maria said. "Papa would sit with us around the fire, singing and telling stories. He built us a playhouse and taught us how to sail. He was very oriented to his children, very fatherly. As long as we were around him we were happy."

Above, left to right: Martina, Johanna, Hedwig, Werner, Maria, Agathe, Rupert. Facing page: The Nonnberg Abbey (with onion dome) is part of Salzburg's reputation as "Rome of the North."

In 1925, Captain von Trapp discussed a move from Vienna to Salzburg. The older children remembered the beauty of Salzburg well; they had traveled there with their mother from Zell-am-See for errands and dentist appointments. They knew that Salzburg was one of Austria's most glorious cities, a place of high mountain peaks, lakes, and the Salzach River.

Salzburg spread out on both banks of the Salzach ("Salt River"). A medieval fortress towered over the city, sentinel-like, from its perch atop the Festungsberg. With a turn of the head, one could see the Kapuzinerberg ("Capuchin Mountain") and the Monchberg ("Monk's Mountain"). In the distance, even loftier peaks rose to the skies. South

Mozart's birthplace, a point of pilgrimage for music lovers in Salzburg.

Villa Trapp in Aigen.

of town, the Untersberg topped 6,000 feet; marble from the mountain was quarried for many of Salzburg's public buildings and churches.

Salzburg's architecture combined Gothic, Romanesque, Baroque, and Rococo styles. The winding streets opened onto broad squares. The city was home to the world-famous Salzburg Music Festival, where the greatest names in the musical world appeared. It seemed that on every street corner aspiring students practiced and performed. Presiding over all this music was the legend of Salzburg's most famous son, Wolfgang Amadeus Mozart. The house where the composer was born in 1756 still stood at Getreidegasse no. 9.

The residence near Salzburg which Captain von Trapp bought for his family was a fifteen-minute bus ride from Cathedral Square. The Villa Trapp was a large, handsome grey mansion with green shutters. It stood on a shady country road at the foot of Gaisberg Mountain, in the village of Aigen. The grounds were wooded and lush, with a barn and outbuildings and a laundry house. At the rear of the estate a gate led out to the Aigen railway station, where trains stopped en route to Salzburg and points beyond.

The von Trapps settled into their newly remodeled twenty-two room home during the fall of 1925. A kindly and refined baroness was engaged to manage the household, and life in Aigen-bei-Salzburg resumed its orderly pattern. The girls entered the Ursuline convent school, while Rupert and Werner enrolled at the public school. Transportation was mainly on foot or by bicycle. "We had a car," Rupert joked, "but most of the time it didn't work!"

In 1926, Maria showed signs of exhaustion, and it became necessary to remove her from school to recuperate. The Captain was concerned that Maria's studies would suffer, so he sought out a tutor who could live in and assist his daughter with lessons. He learned that a qualified teacher was available from the Nonnberg

Abbey in Salzburg. She was a twenty-one year old novice from Vienna, Maria Augusta Kutschera.

Maria Kutschera was a strong, intelligent, lively person who had overcome an early life of hardship. Soon after Maria's birth on January 26, 1905, her mother, Augusta Rainer Kutschera, died. Her father, Karl Kutschera, could not care for the infant daughter, so she was taken to live with a kindly, elderly cousin.

Yet her circumstances soon changed. Maria said, "When I was six, my father died. I had no near relatives, so the court handed me over to a guardian. This guardian happened to be a passionate socialist. The socialists we had at that time in Austria were very close to communists of today. As such, he was a violent anti-Catholic. Suddenly God was out of my life. All the Bible stories which I had loved in my early childhood were now branded as silly legends. So, although I was baptized, I grew up really outside of the Church, hearing nothing but hateful things about it, growing into the same hatred of God and divine things as my surroundings constantly emanated."

The strictness of her guardian, "Uncle Franz," and the lack of a warm family life transformed Maria into a youthful cynic. But her environment fostered her strong will and her desire for an education. As a scholarship student, she entered Vienna's State Teachers College for Progressive Education. The pedagogy of the school was liberal and

Maria Kutschera's confirmation photo. Over: Villa Trapp in Aigen.

seemed to mirror what was happening in Austria in the aftermath of World War I. Gone were the Habsburg emperors; Austria was a republic. But the war had exhausted Austria, and especially in big cities, like Vienna, shortages and hunger abounded.

Young Maria Kutschera was assisted by The Society of Friends. "The famine had gotten so terrible that it was impossible to study or

Maria Kutschera as a student.

Vienna, you really didn't need money to hear good music," she said. "At eight o'clock, you go to the Jesuit church to hear a mass by Mozart. At nine o'clock, you walk around another corner to hear a mass by Haydn. At ten o'clock sharp, you go to the Cathedral of St. Stephen's to hear a mass by Palestrina. At eleven-thirty, you better run. The Imperial Chapel is still in action: the Vienna Philharmonic and the Vienna Choir Boys perform a mass. That's what I did every Sunday; I picked my concerts."

At one of those church services, Maria said she was "thrown off her horse, by a special mercy of God." A famous theologian preached so effectively about salvation through Christ that her interest was piqued. At a later encounter with the priest, Maria refound her Catholic faith, wholeheartedly so. She was then in her final year of college.

During her student days, Maria became involved with a Catholic youth movement called "Neuland." The group banded together for outings in the countryside, playing volleyball, and singing. On hikes through rural Austria, authentic folk music was discovered and adopted by the group; in towns and villages, Neuland gave impromptu concerts. These activities, along with the sense of belonging, appealed to Maria and made a great impact on her. By this time, she was known as "Gustl." With an abundance of Marias and Mitzis all over Austria, her friends simply bor-

do any work," she said. "In the most crucial moment, The Society of Friends came to Vienna with food, and every student and every schoolchild got one hot meal a day. If it had not been for that one hot meal, I might not have lived."

Something other than food fed Maria's soul: music. Vienna was a grand place to indulge in culture, even in those meager years of the early 1920s. "In

rowed "Gustl" from her middle name, Augusta.

After graduation, Gustl was with a group on a hiking trip in the Alps. "I was 8,500 feet up in the mountains," she said, "standing on the edge of a cliff overlooking a whole glacier field being illuminated by a magnificent sunset. I was so overwhelmed by this sight; I thought to myself that God had given this magnificence to me and I wondered what I could give back to Him. As I thought about it the idea came to me to give back to Him all I saw at that glorious moment by entering a strict convent which would deprive me of ever seeing it again."

Impetuous and strong-willed as ever, Maria Augusta Kutschera descended the mountains and took the train to Salzburg. Asking her way around, she landed at the Nonnberg Convent—a strict one, she had been told—and presented herself as a candidate for the novitiate of the Benedictine sisterhood.

She had come to the right place. There was so much ecclesiastical life in Salzburg that it was called the "Rome of the North." Monasteries, abbeys, churches, and the cathedral tolled their many bells daily, adding to the pervasive religious flavor of the city. Bishop Rupert had founded the city in 696, when he arrived as a missionary. He originated the Monastery of St. Peter and the Nonnberg Abbey.

When Maria first ascended the 144 steps leading to the cloistered Nonnberg Abbey, she car-

ried a rucksack and ice picks from her mountain-climbing adventures. The tiny, frail Reverend Mother Abbess accepted this unlikely tomboy into the community. The transformation of the independent tomboy into a pious postulant was a long process. "First

Above left: Nonnberg Abbey door. Above right: Inside the Abbey. Below: Nonnberg outerwall.

27

Above: Courtyard at Nonnberg, with PAX inscription. The arched entrance leads to the convent church where Maria and the Captain were married.

Left: Maria left the cloistered life of Nonnberg to start a new life with the von Trapps.

to make a girl out of a boy, and then to make a nun out of that," as Maria recalled. She taught, grew accustomed to the regulated beauty of convent life, and accepted the belief that "The only important thing on earth is to find out the will of God and do it." When the Reverend Mother Abbess called in her postulant and asked her to leave Nonnberg temporarily, to teach one of Captain von Trapp's children, Maria's reaction was that she didn't want to go. But she also believed that "we have been created by God for a special job, a special plan, a special place."

With her few possessions and a hastily found dress, Maria emerged from Nonnberg for what she thought would be ten months. She made her way to the impressive portal of a sea captain's villa in Aigen and stepped into a new life with the von Trapp family.

Although her role was to be young Maria's tutor, she quickly bonded with all seven children. She seemed like a big sister, telling interesting stories, playing games, answering questions, and joining in with their singing. Of course she shared the songs she knew from her Neuland days.

As the months passed and time grew near for Maria to return to Nonnberg, no one wanted to see her go—including the Captain. He envisioned this young, lively aspiring nun, so full of fun, faith, and music, as a second wife and mother. Maria, at first shocked by this proposal, and torn by her love for the von Trapps and her desire for convent life, was

advised by Reverend Mother to marry. "We prayed to the Holy Spirit," Reverend Mother explained, "and we found it is the will of God that you marry the father of the children."

And so, on November 26, 1927, at Nonnberg Abbey, Maria Augusta Kutschera and Captain Georg von Trapp were married. The nuns sang, the seven children were present, and the wedding, as the bride remembered, was "very, very, very beautiful."

Top: The wedding party, led by the Captain and Maria. Above left: The altar at Nonnberg Abbey, where the Captain and Maria were married. Above right: The new baroness.

CHAPTER 3

A Family of Singers

Maria was 22 when she became the second wife of the Captain and mother to his children. "I have to do my best in becoming a substitute," she thought at the time. Later, she reflected, "At 22, you think nothing of marrying a man with seven children. Georg came with them, almost like a package deal. It took a while for me to mature into him." Captain von Trapp was 47 at the time of his remarriage, twenty-five years his bride's senior.

For Maria, the role of second wife and mother was one she took seriously. She became "Mother" in the family circle, to differentiate from the children's own "Mama." "Mother" read books about second families, trying to avoid any "stepmother" mistakes. She also needed to learn the overseeing of a household, a formidable task for one who had lived in boarding schools and a convent, where meals and housekeeping were not her concern. "The whole thing was overwhelming at first, a household in high style," Maria remembered. But her husband was patient and helpful—"so very, very kind, and understanding," as his wife recalled.

Following Maria's marriage to the Captain, two daughters were added to the family circle. From left: Johanna, Maria, Agathe, Werner, Rosmarie, Rupert, Hedwig, Eleonore, and Martina. Facing page: The church at Maria Plein was a favorite place of pilgrimage for the von Trapps.

The seven children completely accepted Maria as their second mother. Her lively ways, her outgoing personality, and her curiosity about the world around her commanded their attention. She assisted them with their schoolwork, encouraged their interests, and shared her own passionate loves with her new family. Hiking in the mountains, volleyball, and singing—all carryovers from Maria's Neuland experiences—became Trapp family activities.

Of all the influences Maria brought to the children, music was the favored pastime. "They were very musical," Maria said. "So I made sure that one sang first part, one sang second part, and so on. I sang third part, and it sounded beautiful!" Very soon, the Trapp family learned a long list of madrigals and folk songs.

Family firesides in the evenings at Villa Trapp were filled with music making. The Captain played the first violin, and instructed Rupert and Maria on accordion. Agathe learned guitar, and the younger girls studied violin. Of those first music-making experiences, Agathe said, "It was simply part of the climate of our lives. Children of our social standing learned the arts; it was just *done*. You learned music; you learned to draw. In our family, we learned what the others did, and the arts were cherished."

Of his siblings' aptitude for music, Rupert reflected, "As far back as my memory can take me, I

An early photo of the singing family. From left: Johanna, Agathe, Martina, Maria, Hedwig, Mother, Werner, and Rupert.

always loved music. I began piano lessons when I was five; my sister Agathe was soon learning piano, and Maria started both piano and violin. Eventually we began to play together—sonatas and some of the easier chamber music of Handel, Haydn, Corelli, and so on. At the home of relatives, the Auerspergs, at Schloss Goldegg, I remember hearing the great Hungarian pianist, Lily Kraus. Also, there was the Galimar Quartet . . . In those days, there

was a lot of music, especially in people's homes."

Besides their music, the von Trapp children discovered other interests to pursue. Rupert decided to become a doctor at the age of ten; Maria thought of mission work even as a young girl. Agathe's artistic talent was recognized by her father, who arranged for her to study with an Italian watercolor artist. Each of the others—Werner, Hedwig, Johanna, and Martina—excelled in artistic pursuits, in addition to singing and playing instruments.

There were two new additions to the Trapp family, both baby girls, and both welcomed heartily by their seven brothers and sisters. Maria's first daughter was born in February 1929 and named Rosmarie Erentrudis. Two years later, in May 1931, another dark-eyed girl was born and named Eleonore. The girls, who were nicknamed Illi and Lorli, fell eventually under the direction of Hedwig, who was excellent in dealing with children.

In the summer months, the von Trapps' hometown was crowded with music aficionados who convened for the Salzburg Festival. Since 1920, Max Reinhardt's Salzburg Music Festival had annually expanded its scope and reputation. The medieval morality play *Jedermann* (*Everyman*) became a fixture, performed open-air on the Cathedral square. Other performances included Mozart operas, *Fidelio* (with the great soprano Lotte Lehmann), the Vienna Philhar-

monic, Toscanini conducting selected operas—these attractions helped establish the Festival as a world-class event.

Villa Trapp was prime rental property during the Festival, so often the family made summer sojourns to the Adriatic sea during that time, renting out their big house to celebrities or music lovers. Camping, hiking, and sailing were Trapp family summer activities. The Captain enjoyed being commanding officer to his family crew on sailing trips in the Adriatic Sea. "All the children have learned something about sailing a ship," he said proudly.

For one trip, the Captain ordered "fold-boats" made for sailing on the Adriatic. The family visited Pola, the former Austrian harbor town, and camped on the island of Veruda. With their experienced and enthusiastic sailor-father as teacher, the von Trapp children learned to expertly maneuver the fold-boats.

Another summer the family embarked on a longer sail, aboard a native cargo vessel called *Archimede*. This cruise took them along the coast of Istria, Dalmatia, and to the Bocche di Cattaro.

Chamber music, performed on old instruments. Overleaf: "Wherever there are mountains, people sing," remarked Maria von Trapp. Below: Design by Agathe von Trapp.

A Tribute to my Homeland of Austria
by Agathe von Trapp

Austria is a wonderfully beautiful country. It is the heart of Europe. It is the crossroads from the North to the South, from East to West, and West to East. It has seen the hordes of the Huns, the armies of the Romans and Turks, the armies of Napoleon, the Prussians and the Russians on their quest for world domination.

Austria has assimilated from these different invaders something of their languages, their substance, their cultures, and something for almost every aspect of life. Austria has been robbed and pilfered, and yet it survived and stood there on its feet, strong like the mountains, the plains and the lakes that make up its territory. Austria knows how to be rich and how to be poor, how to be proud and how to be humble, how to associate and how to assimilate and how to cast forth. Austria knows how to accumulate and how to suffer loss.

It had an exceptional navy and a determined and self-sacrificing army. It always answered the call, it gave what had to be given and it did what had to be done. It is a country of con-

trasts, of mirth and generosity. It has seen and understood.

Austria had its great men and women. Its composers, musicians and orchestras, its poets and writers, its philosophers, scientists and inventors, its doctors, teachers, merchants and businessmen. It has a unique peasant population. It is a colorful country. it dances and sings and sighs and keeps going. "Austri Erit In Orbe Ultima!" It has a sense of the eternal, of never failing in spite of great odds. It fights to the end and rises from its ashes. It is a blessed country.

Austria has its great architects and its humble women, its institutions of learning, its great men of valour. It has its domes, its cathedrals, monuments and museums. Austria has a glorious past and a promising future. It is a country that charms and warms and thrills. It makes you laugh and cry, because for every situation it has a fitting joke. It thrives on its own sense of humour and will not pass up a situation that can be made into a matter of laughter or into a song.

Austria is a queen and will never be anything less.

(Originally published in Austria Today)

Top: The church at Aigen. Above: Dr. Franz Wasner, conductor and composer for the Trapp Family Choir.

The gracious Villa Trapp became the key to earning extra income. Treating the money loss with a sense of adventure, the family good-naturedly rearranged rooms to allow for paying boarders. Several of the girls were experts in homemaking skills, so they committed to help run the house in place of paid helpers. Rupert was in medical school at Innsbruck, but he later remembered the long-term boarders, among them university professors and a social worker. At this time, one of the rooms of the house was transformed into a chapel, and a chaplain was assigned to say Mass there.

Singing for Mass, either in their own chapel or at the Aigen village church down the road, was a delight for the von Trapps. "When you sing, you pray twice," their stepmother told them. At Easter 1935, a young priest named Franz Wasner said Mass at the Villa Trapp. The family sang, and at breakfast, he commented on their work. "They were remarkable singing in four parts," he noted, "with a natural sound that only members of one family can achieve." Because he was an eminent musician, he began to critique the informal family choir.

Father Wasner appeared at the Villa Trapp at a strategic time. Musically, he was the mentor the family needed to transform their love of group singing to a higher

Much to his delight, the Captain showed his family the beauties of the Mediterranean, where he first learned to love the sea during his youth.

The summer sailing trips planted a dream within the family. Eventually they planned to build a schooner and cruise to the South Seas. But these plans came to a halt in 1932. Suddenly, the family fortune was lost.

The financial depression that sapped America also extended worldwide, and when the Lammer Bank in Zell-am-See failed, the von Trapp money went with it. Rupert said, "I have no idea how much there was, and how much was left; my father never talked about that. But something was left, because we stayed in the house."

degree of excellence. Father Wasner was the son of a farming family from Feldkirchen, in Upper Austria. Following his theological studies at the University of Innsbruck, he was ordained to the priesthood in 1929. He served a parish in the Tyrol before studying ecclesiastical law in Rome, where he was organist at the Austrian National Church. After graduating *summa cum laude* in 1934, he came to Salzburg with his doctorate in canon law. When the thirty-year-old priest met the von Trapps, he was teaching Gregorian chant in the Seminarium Majus in Salzburg.

Father Wasner liked what he heard of the pure, untrained voices of the seven von Trapps and their stepmother. His coaching sessions became rehearsals as he introduced the group to the works of the sixteenth, seventeenth, and eighteenth centuries. For the chapel, they learned motets and masses by Lassus, Vittoria, and Palestrina. Music by Mozart, Haydn, Handel, Isaac, and Thomas Morley followed. Father Wasner was an expert arranger, so he wrote settings of wonderful old folk music, and ballads for the singers. "He insisted that we learn everything by heart, so we could concentrate on the music and not on a paper in our hands," said Maria. The sessions with Father Wasner were simply for the joy of singing. The family members, who had always enjoyed a close unity, sang to praise God and to fulfill a musical urge within. "We just wanted to sing all the time,"

Agathe said of those days when the choir was first formed.

The family's vocal mix was perfect for an *a capella* choir. Agathe and Johanna sang first soprano, and Maria and Martina sang second soprano. Baroness von Trapp had a lovely, mellow alto. Hedwig also sang alto, Werner sang tenor, and Rupert sang bass.

Since much of the music the family liked was written for early instruments, the von Trapps learned to play recorders, those wooden, flute-like instruments popular in the 1500s and 1600s. A

Art by Agathe von Trapp.

The Trapp Family Choir, circa 1936, with their villa at Aigen in the background.

recorder revival started around 1920, along with renewed interest in Renaissance and Baroque music. Along with Werner on his viola da gamba, and Father Wasner on the spinet, the von Trapps had their own chamber music group. Without knowing it, and still dedicated simply to home musicmaking, the von Trapps achieved professional caliber.

In the summer of 1936, Lotte Lehmann came to visit Villa Trapp. She overheard the family singing in their garden, and listened, transfixed. She confronted the von Trapps, telling them they had "gold in their throats" and that a family choir was unique. She urged them to enter a song competition during the Salzburg Festival. Despite the fact that the Captain cringed at the thought of his wife and children singing on a stage, he agreed to "only one time."

Drawing upon the rich repertoire Father Wasner had helped them build, and with his eloquent hands directing them, the von Trapps sang at the competition and won a prize. Lotte Lehmann was delighted. "May the Trapp Choir be destined to a successful future!" she said. "In harmony with the traditions and high expectations of this festival city, Salzburg, it may be anticipated that wherever they go they will reveal, through their singing, the soul of the folk to whom they are so intimately related."

The "Salzburg Trapp Choir" started receiving invitations to perform, and the Captain's "only one time" was forgotten. A hobby became a profession. Captain von Trapp overcame his negative feelings about his family appearing in public and supported them wholeheartedly. He accompanied the family on all appearances, tended to backstage details, and was introduced on stage during the performances.

An invitation to sing at a state affair in Vienna from Austrian chancellor Kurt von Schuschnigg brought the von Trapps to Belvedere Palace in December 1936. "These were years of great experiences for me, that I would not have otherwise had," said Father Wasner of the choir's early performances. A critic in Vienna commented favorably upon their work, saying, "The singers . . . gave evidence of authority and excellent musicianship. The audience was grateful to hear such charming pieces . . . After the intermission the singers appeared in folk costume . . . the girls now wore the beloved dirndls and the two men appeared in their Steiermark uniforms, much to the pleasure of the Viennese, who

Above and Facing Page: Many of the early folk songs sung by the Trapp Family were collected from the beautiful Austrian countryside.

KAMMERCHOR
TRAPP

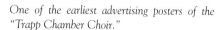

One of the earliest advertising posters of the "Trapp Chamber Choir."

rejoiced and refreshed themselves in the hearty presentation which the singers gave to their mountain calls."

During the 1937 Salzburg Festival, the von Trapps were a distinguished feature, performing at the Mozarteum. Following their appearances, concert agents from all over Europe, and even far-off America, presented them with contracts for tours. What a sensation in the music world! A concert group comprised of members of a

single family!

The first concert tour of the Trapp Family Choir was scheduled for December 1937. From its start in the garden at Aigen, the music of the family was now heard in France, Belgium, Holland, Italy, Germany, and England. They also sang on the radio, and in London the BBC showcased them on the new broadcasting marvel, television. The concerts were followed by glowing reviews, which Agathe pasted into a scrapbook. "They

A pervasive scene in Salzburg—the Fortress.

called us the lovely miracle of the Trapps," she said. One critic wrote, "Whoever thinks he knows about the heart of Austria and has not heard the Trapp Choir has much to learn."

The family's supporters were sincere, and invitations continued to arrive. Eugene Ormandy, conductor of the Philadelphia Orchestra, urged them to tour America. While in Rome, the von Trapps sang for Mussolini, who asked for two encores. They sang Mozart's "Ave Verum" for Pope Pius XI. In London, Queen Mary received them.

The European concert tour was a combined sightseeing trip, a pilgrimage to holy sights, and a foretaste of life in the musical world for Captain von Trapp's family of singers.

Above: The Mozarteum.

Upper Right: "The Horsepond," where Austrian cavalry once bathed their horses.

Right: The Salzach River divides the historic city of Salzburg.

Festival House.

In Salzburg, arches connect one square to the next.

CHAPTER 4

Salzburg, Austria, Home of the von Trapps

Many scenes in Salzburg show it is still a place of religious life.

Above: Salzburg, with the fortress overlooking the city.

Fountains enhance the architectural beauty of Salzburg.

Overleaf: Salzburg at night. "Salzburg is really like a fairy tale," Maria von Trapp once explained.

AUSTRIA

N

DEUTSCHLAND

BREGENZ

VORARLBERG

LANDECK

ST.ANTON

INNSBRUCK

ZELL-AM-S

TIROL

LIENZ

SA

OST

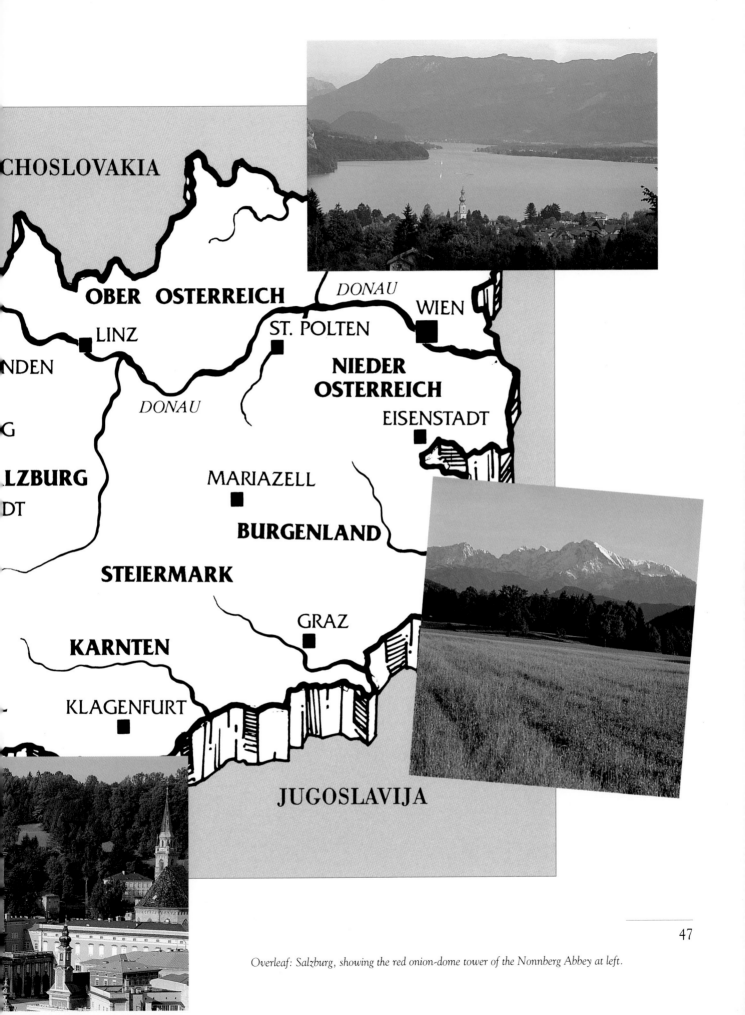

CHOSLOVAKIA

OBER OSTERREICH

LINZ ■

NDEN

G

LZBURG

DT

DONAU

DONAU

ST. POLTEN ■

NIEDER OSTERREICH

WIEN ■

EISENSTADT ■

MARIAZELL ■

BURGENLAND

STEIERMARK

GRAZ ■

KARNTEN

KLAGENFURT ■

JUGOSLAVIJA

47

Overleaf: Salzburg, showing the red onion-dome tower of the Nonnberg Abbey at left.

In 1938 and 1939, the Trapp Family made two trips into the United States following their flight from Hitler-invaded Austria. Here they are in October 1939. Top row: Werner and Rupert. Left to right, middle row: Father Wasner, Johanna, Mother with baby Johannes, Georg, Hedwig, Martina, and Maria. In front: Agathe, Rosmarie, and Eleonore.

CHAPTER 5

For God and Country

Ever since the rise of the Nazis in neighboring Germany, Captain von Trapp had watched the political climate warily. He knew that some of his fellow Austrians favored union with Germany, a thought that greatly disturbed his patriotic sensibilities. Chancellor Dollfus had so strongly opposed a unified Austria and Germany that the Nazis had him killed in 1934. His successor, Kurt von Schuschnigg, continued to keep Austria an independent nation.

On March 11, 1938, the inevitable happened. Nazi boots marched into Austria, and the country was annexed by Germany. Hitler announced the Anschluss (union) of Austria and Germany. As the von Trapps sat listening to the radio in the library at home, they heard bells pealing from every church in nearby Salzburg. The Captain called the police to find out what was happening, and learned that the Nazis had moved into Salzburg. The bells were "welcoming" the conquerors.

"We are standing at the open grave of Austria," Captain von Trapp remarked of the propaganda techniques and tactics used by the Nazis. Although it was best to stay silent about one's beliefs, the von Trapps remained steadfast in their loyalty to the old Austria. Agathe sewed black aprons to be worn by her sisters with their Austrian peasant dresses as a sign of mourning.

In Salzburg, signs of occupation were everywhere. People mysteriously disappeared; in the schools, teachers were replaced by those indoctrinated with Nazi party beliefs. In every cafe, on every street, the "Heil Hitler" salute was heard. Nazi flags hung everywhere, and every household was expected to display this symbol of evil. The Villa Trapp was no exception.

The Captain said, "When they sent us a big silk Nazi flag, we refused to hang it out our window. They called me to their headquarters and demanded an explanation. I said, 'I'm sorry, but I don't understand what you want us to hang the flag for.' They told me, to show appreciation that the Fuhrer is coming. I said, 'All right, we will

Top: The Captain and children on a mountain expedition. Above: Johanna, Werner, Hedwig, Agathe and Martina.

During the war years, the family kept scrap books of political news and cartoons.

Left: Some of the Trapp daughters enjoy the mountain country near St. Georgen, Italy.

Below: The family at the guest house in St. Georgen, where they waited until the appointed time to leave for America.

The "American Farmer" which carried the Trapp Family from England to America.

Above: The family during the 1938 crossing aboard "The American Farmer".

Far left: S.S. American Farmer passenger list.

Left: Rosmarie and Eleonore.

decorate if you want, but that color doesn't fit our house well. But we have some very fine Oriental rugs we will be glad to hang out the window, if you like.' A few days later they asked us to sing for Hitler's birthday. We refused, and very soon after, we knew we had to go."

The tense situation was heightened by two more Nazi propositions. Maria von Trapp explained, "They offered my husband the command of a German submarine. To our eldest son, Rupert, who was just out of medical college and had barely served his internship, they offered a post as head of one of the great Vienna hospitals. Such a position with its handsome salary would have made it possible for him to support a wife and a home. But we knew that the job they wanted to give Rupert was a job taken from a Jewish doctor, and that if my husband had served the Nazis it would be a compromise with all the ideals that meant so much to us. There was not an instant's doubt in any of our minds. Exile and persecution would be preferable."

When their trusted butler Hans showed them the swastika on his lapel, the von Trapps knew that they had a Nazi in their home. He implored them not to openly criticize the new regime in his presence; he would have to report such talk to the Gestapo. But the family's sentiments already were known; when they tried to rent concert halls, they found each one mysteriously booked and unavailable. As Maria said, "It was

either stay and say 'Heil Hitler', or get out."

Lotte Lehmann declared that she would never sing for the Nazis, and she activated a contract to sing in America. Her advice to the Trapp Family was to do the same, and fortunately, they had such an offer. During the 1937 Salzburg Festival season, a concert impresario from New York named Charles L. Wagner visited Villa Trapp and offered the family a tour in America. This became their ticket out of Austria.

The Captain handled the decision in a fatherly, diplomatic fashion. He gathered the family and asked them one by one if they were willing to leave. Each said yes. Then, to seek God's confirmation, he opened the Bible and let a pencil fall at random on a page. The words from Genesis said: "And the Lord said to Abram: Leave thy country and thy people, go out of thy father's house and come into the land which I shall show thee."

During the summer of 1938, the family quietly made plans. Father Wasner, so essential to the choir, was given permission by the Archbishop of Salzburg to accompany them. His editorship of an anti-Nazi Catholic newspaper placed him in jeopardy. The Villa Trapp was entrusted to priests of the nearby Boromaeum which had been taken over by the Nazis.

Through the days of preparation, the family felt completely within the will of God. Eleonore explained, "The family, as a whole and with the individuals' consent,

Lotte Lehmann

A Talent Scout Remembers

Agathe von Trapp credits Nelly Walter with discovering the Trapp Family's potential for touring in America. Her introductions resulted in performance contracts. In 1992, Nelly Walter recalled: "It was I who discovered the Trapp Family when I was in Vienna before Hitler marched in. I asked the great Mr. Coppicus who came regularly to Europe because he was interested in our great stars, to do me the favor and listen to the Trapps. I even took a special hall for this audition. His reaction was "How can you imagine that I can bring them to New York with that kind of attire?" (The whole family wore Tyrolean peasant outfits). I was very disappointed since the Trapps had come to Vienna at their own expense and money was very tight with them. I quickly asked my dear friend Charlie Wagner who engaged just about everything I presented to him to do me the great favor to make the trip to Salzburg which would be very much worth his while. I took a horse carriage to show him all the historical points of Salzburg and drove him to the Trapp castle. . .Wagner was enchanted with the Trapps' performance and immediately engaged them . . ."

Maria von Trapp

consecrated itself to the Sacred Heart of Jesus. God accepted this consecration and made us His very own special family." The certainty that came with this trust in God led daughter Maria to say, "I never once worried if the choir would be a success in America. And we knew *nothing* about America, only that there were cowboys, gangsters, and skyscrapers!"

Although the von Trapps were Austrians, a technicality made them Italian citizens. Trieste, their former home, became part of Italy after World War I, so they had Italian citizenship and passports. This enabled them to leave Austria freely, on the guise of a vacation to the Dolomite country of South Tyrol. On an August morning, the family quietly left home, each with one suitcase and one rucksack. They boarded the train at the

Aigen station and headed for St. Georgen in northern Italy. With their Italian passports, the Nazis could do them no harm.

The family spent several weeks at a guest house in the mountains. They went mountain climbing, they rehearsed on a rigorous schedule, and they prayed. There was much to pray about: the shaky peace of the world, their own future in a strange country, and the fact that a new baby was expected. A doctor had warned the Captain and Maria that her pregnancy was a precarious one.

Early in October, the family boarded the *American Farmer* on its Southampton to New York voyage, with tickets advanced by the American concert manager. When they arrived in New York and checked into the Wellington Hotel, they scraped up four dollars between them. "We were the poorest of the poor—refugees," Maria said of those first days when her husband and children landed, not knowing English, with no money, no friends, and no home.

But they knew God was with them. The family coat of arms declared: "Nec aspera terrent" ("Let nothing difficult frighten thee.") Each day was a challenge as they struggled with the language and absorbed new customs. Immediately they were sent off for the concert tour, traveling by bus.

The first American concert of the Trapp Family Choir was at Easton, Pennsylvania. The audience responded well to the program of Bach, Mozart, Brahms, and other masters. The instrumen-

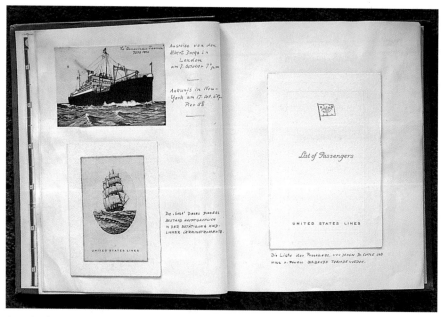

Scrapbooks were kept of concerts, travels and sightseeing.

tal section was applauded, even though the ancient recorder was little known in America. The Austrian yodels and folk songs, sung in native costume, were a sensation. And though they spoke not one word from the stage, to everyone's surprise they sang "My Old Kentucky Home" in perfect English.

The tour, which went as far west as Oklahoma, introduced the family not only to the landscape, but also to the friendliness of Americans. Everywhere they went, people were fascinated with their native costumes, their lives, and their singing. Newspapers and magazines found them intriguing subjects, often asking the Captain to comment on conditions in Europe. He was reticent to make any war predictions, and instead would say, "In Europe, the name of Austria is lost. We are trying to show the Austrian life and customs are not lost."

For the Baroness Maria, the concert trip was challenging with a baby on the way. To conceal that fact, she had a series of costumes made to mask her condition. Her dressmaker told her that a padded bosom, in graduated sizes, would achieve the needed effect. As the months went on, the newspapers described her as ample, then portly, and finally, stately.

Following the introductory tour, the Trapp Family Choir sang in the prestigious Town Hall in New York City. This New York performance gave the group important exposure to critics, managers, and music lovers. So spellbinding was

the sight and sound of the singers that Agathe recalled, "Audiences sat as if frozen when we started to sing." *The New York Times* complimented their work highly, and added that "there was something unusually lovable about this little group."

Their music attracted their first new friends in America. When the first tour was over, friends banded together to find a house for the family in the Philadelphia suburb of Germantown. Rosmarie and Eleonore, who had been placed in a boarding school, rejoined the family.

Maria von Trapp shortly before the flight from Austria. The family gives her much credit for forging ahead with plans and creativity which enabled them to make a successful start in America. Below left: The Wellington Hotel in New York City was located near Carnegie Hall. It lodged the Trapp Family when they first arrived in New York City, and was headquarters during many subsequent stops in the metropolis.

The family was billed as the "Salzburg Trapp Choir" on their first tour.

THE SALZBURG
TRAPP CHOIR

Management CHARLES L. WAGNER, INC.
511 FIFTH AVENUE   NEW YORK, N.Y.

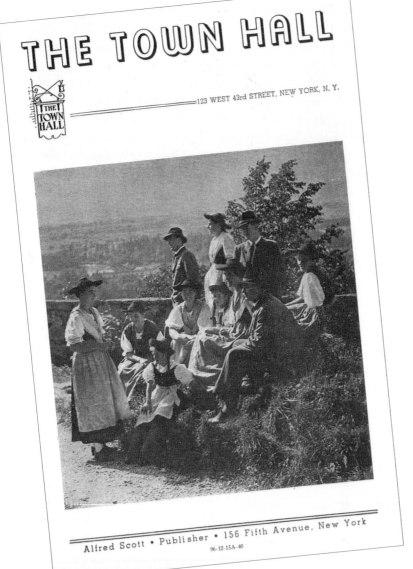

THE TOWN HALL

123 WEST 43rd STREET, NEW YORK, N. Y.

Alfred Scott • Publisher • 156 Fifth Avenue, New York

96-12-15A-40

In their new temporary home the day started with Father Wasner's mass in the morning; then there were the usual rehearsals. Housekeeping chores were divided among the girls. Germantown residents soon grew used to seeing the family on trolleys, in the station, and in the stores.

The tenth and last von Trapp child was born during the sojourn in Germantown; on January 17, 1939 Johannes Georg appeared. This was an occasion of celebration: the first American-born von Trapp! But soon after, the family was forced to return to Europe when their American visitor's visas expired. It was impossible to return to Austria, so they purchased tickets for Scandinavia, where there were promises of concerts.

Fifty-six performances throughout Denmark, Sweden and Norway transpired during the spring and summer. Some family members made a short, stealthy visit to Austria. Seeing their country under Nazi domination cured

STUDENT TICKET
Good for Two Seats
TOWN HALL
Sat. Aftn., Dec. 10 at 3 p.m.

STUDENT TICKET (NO TAX)
This ticket will entitle bearer to one (or two) Orchestra seat(s) at 25c each, or one (or two) Balcony seat(s) at 15c each for the concert of
THE TRAPP FAMILY CHOIR and YELLA PESSL, Harpsichordist
Town Hall, Sat. aftn., Dec. 10th at 3 p.m.
Present at Town Hall Box Office up to 2:00 P.M. day of concert, or at Steinway Box Office, 113 West 57th Street, up to noon the day of concert.
WILL NOT BE HONORED AFTER 2:00 DAY OF CONCERT
Management: Edith Behrens, 63 West 56th Street, N. Y. C.

Top: Town Hall in New York City was a prestigious venue for performers. The family sang there regularly throughout their career on stage. Left: The Trapp Family Choir. Above: Yella Pessl joined the family for the debut concert at Town Hall.

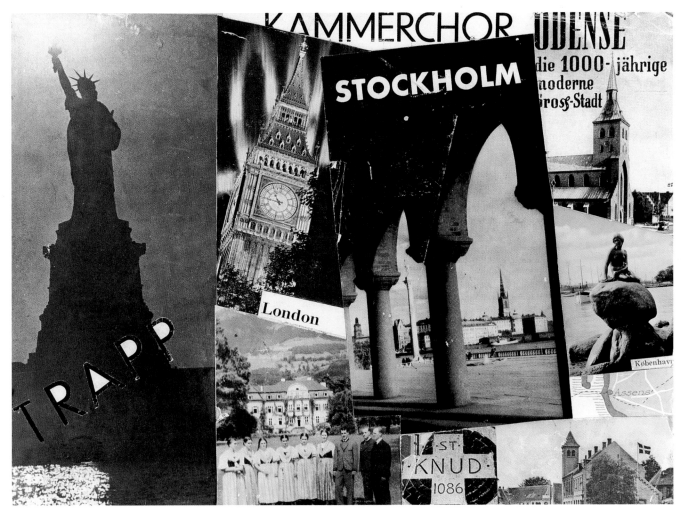

The family's return to Europe in 1939 included a Scandinavian tour.

them of homesickness. "It was all hypocrisy," Maria von Trapp declared. "They told people they could go to church, and if they did, they lost their jobs. Children were forbidden to tell their parents what they learned in school. There were shortages everywhere. We had done the right thing by leaving."

The summer of 1939 was a tense one, as Europe hovered on the brink of war. In some places, the Trapp family was suspected of being Nazi spies. They were living on a Swedish lakeside when Germany attacked Poland and World War II broke out. The fam-

ily then joined the many throngs who hastened to find ship passage back to America.

The ship they found, which Maria von Trapp declared "a first cousin to Noah's ark," neverthe-less sailed safely across the Atlantic and arrived on October 7, 1939. "My husband could bare-ly stop me from kneeling down and kissing the ground of America," Maria said. Her exuber-ance led her to make an unwise comment when an immigration officer asked how long she planned to remain in the United States. "I hope forever," was her earnest reply. This innocent com-

Ellis Island, in sight of the Statue of Liberty, is now restored as a national landmark. Many now-famous immigrants were once held there.

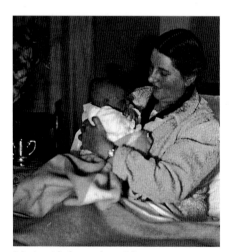

Maria with the newborn Johannes.

ment made the entire group suspect. They were placed at Ellis Island, the immigration processing center in New York Harbor.

It was three days before friends and Catholic church officials could intervene and secure the von Trapps' release. The family made the best of the interlude by singing, playing recorders, and yodelling, all of which delighted fellow immigrants. When they were finally safe on American soil, they took out their first papers for citizenship.

The second tour of the Trapp Family Choir continued the Americanization process, assisted by a bus-driver who was determined to educate the greenhorns from Austria. Rigid economy was practiced, with budget hotels and cheap cafes the routine. The family members struggled to learn more English, spent long hours in rehearsal and endless hours on the bus as their second tour crisscrossed the countryside to such places as Bowling Green, Ohio; Elmhurst, Illinois; and Fort Wayne, Indiana.

Wherever they went, the choir was well received musically. The director of the Music

WESTERN UNION

CLASS OF SERVICE
This is a full-rate Telegram or Cablegram unless its deferred character is indicated by a suitable symbol above or preceding the address.

R. B. WHITE
PRESIDENT
NEWCOMB CARLTON
CHAIRMAN OF THE BOARD
J. C. WILLEVER
FIRST VICE-PRESIDENT

The filing time shown in the date line on telegrams and day letters is STANDARD TIME at point of origin. Time of receipt is STANDARD TIME at point of destination

Received at 1414 Sixth Avenue, New York

NAJ154 14=HA WASHINGTON DC 12 317P   039 OCT 12 PM 4 22

GEORGE VON TRAPP WELLINGTON HOTEL=

7 AVE AND 55=

DEPARTMENT OF LABOR HAS ADMITTED YOU AND ENTIRE GROUP

FOR SIX MONTHS AS VISITORS=

BRUCE M MOHLER NATIONAL CATHOLIC WELFARE

CONFERENCE=

Prominent American friends and acquaintances vouched for the family, which resulted in their release from Ellis Island.

Department at Phillips Academy in Andover, Massachusetts wrote to Manager Charles Wagner that "the audience was delighted with the Trapp Choir . . . The performance of this family is so unique that I hope you will not allow the programme to be cheapened in the slightest degree. Keep this group going, and let them realize the highest ideals."

Their high ideals and staunch belief that God guided them led Captain von Trapp and his family through the tumultuous events of 1938 and 1939. In their voluntary exile they encountered danger and difficulty until they were settled in America. They knew well the meaning of the proverb "Aller anfang ist schwer"—"Every new beginning is hard." But with their music, their faith, and their unity, the transplanted family weathered the storm and took root in a new land.

The TRAPP FAMILY SINGERS

"An Evening of Joyous Song"　　　　　　　　　　Dr. Franz Wasner, Conductor

Photo Elisofon

A MUSICAL MIRACLE . . . because they have made successful concert tours for the past five years in as many countries . . . because they have been everywhere acclaimed for their flawless musicianship, their perfect pitch and warm vocal color . . . but chiefly because, as finished artists, they still retain that same youthful exuberance and spontaneity in singing which has made friends for them all over the world.

A PROGRAM to give hardened concert-goers a new thrill: a-capella singing of the great classic composers; a group played on blockflutes, viol di gamba and spinet; and lusty folk songs, mountain calls and yodels, brought from the happy traditions of their own homeland, and given in colorful native costumes.

adoption of showmanship to bring you en rapport with audiences. I really believe you have solved your problem and urge you to expand and continue your explanations."

From Denver on, the sincerity of the Trapp Family Singers endeared them to their audiences. "We have just pushed out one wall of our living room at home and are singing to you as if we were in our own home," the Baroness explained to concertgoers. She assumed the rule of hostess on the stage and commentator during the concerts. The role suited her well; she was a natural storyteller, with a subtle sense of humor. Even her Austrian accent pleased the audience. "Mother had great imagination, and knew how to make things go well on stage," said Agathe.

The concerts of the Trapp Family Singers made musical history. As the stage curtains parted, a hush fell over the audience who had never experienced a concert by a singing family. The five girls filed on, wearing formal gowns of white silk, with black and gold brocade bodices. The two brothers came on in Austrian-style suits. The Baroness wore a black taffeta gown, and like the daughters, her hair was pulled back plainly with braids coiled in back. Father Wasner conducted the choir in an opening selection of sacred music, which might include beautiful masterpieces by Bach, Palestrina, Orlando di Lassus, or Gregorian chant.

"Everyone who performs has some stage fright, but we never had very much of it," Rupert said of the concertizing. "We simply felt people would like what we did, and they did!" The initial sight and sound of the family on stage seemed to create a profound aura which continued throughout the performance. Eleonore, who was not on stage during the first years, but later performed for ten seasons, marveled at the audience reaction. "As soon as we started singing," she said, "we could feel a peace descend on the audience; it was *every* time! God was simply working."

Introductions were made by Baroness von Trapp. "These are my daughters, Agathe, Maria, Hedwig, Johanna, and Martina," she would say. "And my sons, Rupert and Werner; our religious leader and conductor, Reverend Franz Wasner. And I am the mother." Captain von Trapp would emerge from backstage to make a courtly bow as the proud father of the talented family.

Introductions were also necessary for the second portion of the program, which consisted of instrumental music. Few Americans were familiar with the ancient recorders, Werner's viola da gamba, or the spinet. The Baroness explained that the recorder was actually an old-fashioned flute. "My family first started playing the recorder in Austria when we, with

Backstage, before a concert: although the girls shunned the use of makeup in their personal lives, the strong lighting on the stage made it a necessity when performing. "You don't want people to think you're sick, do you?" Freddy Schang asked, as he counseled them on their stage appearance.

Below: "Mother Trapp," storyteller, singer, and group spokesperson.

Werner in the driver's seat.

The family stopped to visit their old friend and supporter Lotte Lehmann in Santa Barbara, California.

The family included stops at missions, convents, and monasteries whenever they could, singing for those in the religious life.

Before tours, the Captain and Maria plotted out the route on a big map posted at home.

ohannes and bus driver.

The bus became a home on wheels for the Trapp Family when they toured. By 1941, they had performed coast-to-coast.

Father Wasner, found so much of the older classical music written for it." Then the family demonstrated different combinations of their instruments—a sonata for one or two recorders with viola da gamba and spinet, or a trio of recorders. Works by Vivaldi, Telemann, Couperin, and L'Oiellet were flawlessly rendered. Occasionally, instruments accompanied the singing, such as the family's version of Bach's "Jesu, Joy of Man's Desiring."

The instrumental selections were followed by madrigals, particularly of Italian and English composers of the fifteenth and sixteenth centuries. The Italian samplings included Orlando de Lassus's "The Soldier's Serenade" and Gastoldi's "Fahren wir froh im Nachen." English madrigals were represented with "Sing We and Chant It," "Now is the Month of Maying," "Sweet Honey-Sucking Bees," and "Lady, your eye my love enforced."

After the madrigals were completed, there was an intermission. The family then changed into their Austrian costumes. The girls wore the "feast-day" dress—black dirndls with colorful aprons and scarves and white, full-sleeved blouses. The boys wore lederhosen, colorful stockings, and silver-buckled shoes. Audible "ohs and ahs" arose from the audience when the curtains opened to this brilliant array of authentic Austrian attire. This set the scene for a lively selection of Austrian folk songs. There were the lusty hunting songs, rollicking nonsense songs, and romantic folk songs of mountain shepherdesses and their sweethearts. Then there were yodels; Werner was a master at this musical form. For the "Echo Yodel," Hedwig disappeared into the wings to provide the appropriate echo effect.

The last segment of the concert featured international folk songs. Wherever they traveled, the family acquired indigenous music, which Father Wasner arranged and incorporated into their performances. Eventually, they sang flawlessly in over a dozen languages, including Latin, Italian, Swedish, Danish, English, Czech, Spanish, Portuguese, French, and a variety of dialects. Finally there were encores, which might include Brahms' "Lullabye."

Following the concerts, people came backstage to visit, or local sponsors held receptions to honor the Trapps. The hour was sometimes late when the family arrived back at their hotel.

Often, an early departure was necessary the following morn-

ing to arrive at the next concert town on time. After mass by Father Wasner, breakfast, and packing, the family was on the road again. They made several tours by car and train, but most often traveled the highways of the United States and Canada in a specially marked bus, labeled TRAPP FAMILY SINGERS. Concert itineraries were not always geographically consistent; scheduling might require detours and returns, which meant hundreds of extra miles of travel. As much as possible the bus was made comfortable, and the family passed the long hours by reading, rehearsing, working at handcrafts, or watching the varied landscape of America pass by. After several days on tour, the Trapps simply became "old troupers"; life on the road was their daily routine.

Long stretches between towns were enlivened by sightseeing. "Mother was fun-loving and interested in seeing the world," Agathe said, "and whenever she could, she arranged sightseeing tours for us." And so the bus stopped at historic sites, natural wonders, and points of interest. Werner said, "We often wished that every schoolchild could have the opportunity to see all the won-

After a long day of travel Agathe, Maria, Hedwig, and Johanna wrote letters to sisters Rosmarie and Eleonore, who remained at home so that their schooling would not be interrupted. Rosmarie always remembered the big packets of mail from the family on tour, and postcards showing the sights they saw en route.

derful places we visited." There were also stops at monasteries and nunneries to sing for those in the religious life.

Upon arriving in the next concert town, work started up again. Often, there were press and radio interviews, photo sessions, and meetings with local sponsors. Some of the members of the family checked out conditions at the concert facility while the others checked into the hotel. Concert equipment was unloaded and set up; costumes were ironed. Captain von Trapp, although he did not sing onstage, tended to details as they arose. His children remember how supportive he was in his quiet way, in a life so different from his intended career.

There were inevitable pitfalls of constant travel: snowstorms that caused delays, forgotten concert luggage, hotel rooms resold during the concerts. The first tours required a stringent budget. Once the family assembled in a hotel dining room to discover that the most economical dinner was a dollar. They all rose *en masse* to seek out a more reasonable cafe.

Eventually, the Trapp Family Singers became Columbia Concerts' greatest group attraction. Their appearances were in

In August 1941, the family visited FBI headquarters. Reviews, feature stories written about them, and souvenirs from their trips were compiled into scrapbooks.

high demand, and their fee rose to $1,000 per concert. The annual tours expanded from 60 performances to 100, and finally to 125. They experienced more return dates than any other group, and finally were dubbed "the most heavily booked attraction in concert history."

Although concertizing was a way to make a living, the Trapp Family Singers sang for another reason. "We know," Eleonore said, "that God had a purpose in our singing, and that is why we kept on; it was that feeling of mission."

Johanna's painting of edelweiss, her father's favorite Austrian flower.

Chapter 7

Life at Home

The Trapp Family Singers performed in Lowell, Massachusetts on Pearl Harbor Day, December 7, 1941. They led the audience in singing "My County 'Tis of Thee" on that fateful Sunday, personally grateful that they were safe in America. "We are so anxious," Maria von Trapp said, "to remind our friends in America of what a privilege it is to live and speak and think and worship as they please."

For the Trapps, America's hospitable attitudes towards newcomers allowed them to earn a living, wear their Austrian clothing, and speak their native language freely. Eventually, they took the first steps to become American citizens. "We feel at home in God's own country," Maria said.

Between concert tours, which ran from fall to spring with an interlude around Christmas, the family returned to Merion, Pennsylvania. Indeed, their rented house in Merion was the only spot the Trapp family could call home, because their villa at Aigen was confiscated by the Nazis. The priests in whose care they had left the place were vacated and renovations were made to accommodate Heinrich Himmler, the Nazi Gestapo head. A massive brick wall enclosed the property, and within lay one of the Nazi seats of power.

Father Wasner conducted daily mass.

Homecoming from tour meant a reunion with Rosmarie and Eleonore, who were either tutored at home or in boarding school while the family traveled. Johannes always traveled with the family with his crib at the rear of the bus.

At home, the family members each assumed a role to keep the big group of fourteen operating as smoothly as it did on stage. There were the twelve Trapps, plus Father Wasner and Maria's friend Martha who had accompanied them to America. Cooking for such a large group was similar to operating a restaurant. This became Johanna's responsibility, since she had been practicing culinary skills for several years. She was an expert chef, producing three hearty meals daily.

Johanna recreated American versions of such Austrian favorites as Leberknodel-Suppe, Wienerschnitzel mit Gurken Salat, Linzertorte, and palatschinken. Martina assisted by waiting on the table. At the end of every meal, the family pronounced the traditional Austrian toast, "Gesegnete Mahlzeit." In the afternoons they sometimes paused for "Jause"—afternoon coffee with cream, and bread and jam or pastries.

Their Austrian dress attracted attention wherever the family went.

Overleaf: The Trapp Family, circa 1941. Seated at left: Rupert; Maria and Johannes, Georg; behind them: Hedwig and Martina. At right: Eleonore and Agathe. Rear: Rosmarie, Maria, Johanna and Werner.

Top: Dinner at home was a welcome event following hurried meals on tour before evening concerts. Above: Johanna collects the daily milk delivery.

Hedwig took over what she called "the ministry of the laundry." Her sisters mended stockings, which might include fifty pairs each week. Rupert and Werner polished shoes each day, and Hedwig learned the skills of shoemaking. The Captain was a fine carpenter. "There is nothing in the house he cannot fix," his wife said proudly. The Baroness answered all the correspondence and acted as the liaison between the family and Columbia Concerts. Father Wasner, in addition to his musical chores, served as the family treasurer.

Agathe was an expert seamstress, so she was responsible for sewing—both making clothing and keeping it in repair. When the family first arrived in America, they decided to retain their Austrian outfits both on stage and off, in order to save money. "Besides," Agathe admitted, "we loved our Austrian dresses." They joked that they were never out of fashion; when hemlines went up or down, theirs remained the same. On tour, gas station attendants and people on the street stared with interest at their Austrian clothing when the family emerged from the bus.

"My older brothers and sisters made a life for themselves, by faith and their own hands," observed Rosmarie of the early years of the family in America. "Everyone had something to offer; it was really a community effort. I see us now as a pioneer family, and that's the greatest legacy I have from my family."

And so, as a cooperative unit, the Trapps lived as the first Christians had, working together and sharing, with each receiving what he or she needed. There were no individual salaries paid for singing; especially in the first years, all the concert income was needed to keep the family afloat. Despite their successes in the concert world, the Trapps were still refugees. "A refugee is not just someone lacking in money and everything else," wrote Maria von Trapp. "A refugee is vulnerable to the slightest touch: he has lost his country, his friends, his earthly belongings. He is a stranger, sick at heart. He is suspicious; he feels misunderstood . . . He is a full-grown tree in the dangerous process of being transplanted, with the chance of possibly not being able to take root in a new soil. As far as we were concerned, our dear Pennsylvania friends took all these feelings away and made us feel secure . . ."

Among those kindly American friends were Henry and Sophie Drinker, who had offered the Trapps the empty house in Merion opposite theirs. At Christmas, unexpected presents arrived from new neighbors and acquaintances. Friends offered advice, answered questions, gave directions, and shared their time.

Johanna, Johannes, and Eleonore created Easter decorations, using an old Austrian peasant tradition.

Art by Johanna von Trapp.

"May God bless all our American friends," daughter Maria said. "They helped us when we were newly arrived in this country and always showed interest in our taking roots and growing in our new home."

The Americanization of the Trapp Family went forth speedily, both on tour and at home. Maria von Trapp observed, "Anyone can come to America, but it is something else to become American, to change your outlook, your attitude, to practice Americanism." One eye-opener was that Americans were proud of humble origins. At a dinner party one evening, a young man

tooled leather goods. Werner was a silversmith, creating jewelry. Martina painted, especially in the Austrian peasant style. Johanna worked in clay. The exhibit of all this accumulated craftsmanship in New York produced orders and sales which kept the family financially afloat until the next concert tour.

In Austria, the family had been accustomed to a rich world of native crafts and the works of skilled artisans. To their surprise, they found such workmanship in America becoming extinct. "You can't have everything ready-made," complained Maria von Trapp. "Life is like a plant; it takes time to develop." Although she was not skilled at handicrafts herself, she was a strong proponent for crafts within families. Between tours, and sometimes even on the bus, the talented Trapp Family sketched, designed, and created.

For fun and amusement, the Trapp children published their own in-house newspaper. An issue was produced in honor of the Captain's sixtieth birthday in April 1940; other issues were filled with humor and caricatures. Father Wasner's recipe for grilled meat and vegetables over an open fire appeared in one issue, with a cartoon of the usually dignified conductor as chef. These newspaper productions were circulated around the family for everyone's enjoyment.

The Trapp Family, who sang together, worked together, and lived together, became an

Agathe's artwork was used to illustrate books and appeared on greeting cards.

sat at Maria's left, wearing formal clothes. The next morning, she saw him delivering coal. Thinking she would spare him embarrassment, she turned her head away. But he called out, "Don't you remember me? At dinner last night?" As she told the family later, "He did not seem a bit ashamed. He said he was learning the business from the ground up."

That same entrepreneurial spirit helped the family during a lean financial period, when they created the "Trapp Family Handicraft Exhibit." "My children are very handy and can do almost anything that can be done by ten fingers," said Maria von Trapp. The children specialized in various folk arts. Agathe painted and sketched, and made exquisite linoleum block prints. Maria was a woodcarver. Hedwig turned out

Left: Martina's folk art decorated trays and bowls, and she hand painted a set of bedroom furniture built by the Captain for Johannes. Above: Werner developed an interest in silversmithing, soon after he arrived in America. Below: Daughter Maria perfected the medium of the monoprint; her work was displayed and sold in Europe and America.

American symbol of solidarity during the bleak years of World War II. Of the flood of European artists and musicians who came to America as refugees, the family's wholesomeness and good cheer made them favorites. Their lives on tour and at home were constantly described in newspapers and magazines. They also sang on numerous popular radio programs including "We, the People" and the "United States Steel Hour." Movie theater newsreels showcased their unique lifestyle.

Over the mantelpiece in the Trapp home in Merion, three flags were placed. Maria von Trapp explained, "One is the flag of our Austria. The second is the flag that we flew from our schooner that we used to sail in the Adriatic. The third is Baby Johannes' flag. And it is the Stars and Stripes." A merging of cultures took root in the Trapp Family. They learned American ways but retained those of their homeland.

Agathe's linoleum print of Cor Unum, the Trapp Family home near Stowe.

Chapter 8

Settling Down in the Green Mountains

When the 1942 concert season ended, the Trapp Family Singers had $1,000 in reserve. Their first difficult days in America were behind them; the initial struggles with language, limited finances, and becoming established as musicians were over. With their newly-earned wealth, the family debated whether to outfit everyone with American clothing, or to invest in a permanent home. Unanimously, they decided that a place of their own in the country was more important.

On tour, whenever the bus crossed a state line, the driver gave a ceremonial three toots of the horn. The first time concerts took the family to Vermont, the driver gave a bleak explanation of the Green Mountain state. "All they raise is tombstones," he said. "Very unprogressive state." But when summer approached, a note arrived from a Mr. Rutledge in Stowe, Vermont, saying, "If you want a vacation, I have a big place in the mountains you may like." The family decided to rent "The Stowe-Away" for the season. The price was right: $100.

That summer among the cool mountains was a nostalgic one for the Trapp Family; on every side, they were reminded of Austria. Up the road from "The Stowe-Away" was Vermont's highest peak, Mount Mansfield, overlooking hills and valleys, forests and lakes. The nearby village of Stowe was one of New England's quaintest towns, first settled in 1794. By the Civil War era, Stowe was a well-known summer resort town because of its natural beauty and peaceful atmosphere.

"Regardless of what our bus driver thought," Maria von Trapp said, "we loved our vacation in Vermont. We hiked everywhere. When there were no hiking trails, we just pushed through all the underbrush and got scratched all over and enjoyed it all immensely. We climbed Round Top and one of the boys scaled a tree to say, 'The view is gorgeous.'

"We had begun talking only among ourselves that maybe we should buy a home in Vermont when a very strange thing happened: real estate people began knocking on our door, saying 'We hear you're interested in buying a place in Vermont.'"

Up and down the state of Vermont, the family investigated prop-

Top: One of Stowe's most familiar landmarks, the Community Church. The building was constructed in 1863. Above: The present Helen Day Library and Art Center was the Stowe high school when the Trapps first came to town.

83

Stowe, Vermont when the Trapp Family first knew it.
Photo: The Vermont Historical Society

Top: The emerging house on the farm, showing the original remaining kitchen ell and the chalet-like addition.

Right: "Uncle Craig Burt," Stowe lumberman, early promoter of the ski industry, and mentor of the Trapps.

Below: Stowe's Town Hall, where the Trapp Family sang a benefit performance for the school. "When the concert was over," Maria said, "we gave an encore and the people applauded like mad. But nobody got the idea the concert was over. So we gave another encore. After the fifth encore, we said, 'This is it!'"

erties, never finding one exactly to their liking. Affordable places were so run-down and rickety that they were hardly inhabitable; better acreages were too costly. As daughter Maria recalled, "Father and Mother drove around Vermont looking for a place to buy. They often returned saying that places announced as 'good condition' were in rotten condition. Finally they found a place near a lake near Brattleboro, in southern Vermont. They put $100 as down payment."

As they often did when important decisions confronted them, the Trapp Family prayed, earnestly seeking God's will for them. For three days and nights, family members took turns praying in a tiny room of "The Stowe-Away." On the last Sunday in Stowe a friend arrived to tell the family of a farm for sale. "Let's go look," Rupert suggested, and family members agreed to take a drive in the beautiful late summer weather to examine the place.

What the family found was a 660-acre tract of land with magnificent views. The glorious panorama included six mountain ranges. Two-thirds of the farmland was mountainous and upland pasture.

"We were in awe at the most beautiful view," Maria said. "We stood on a rock and looked all around—and fell in love with the place. Papa loved it as the horizon was wide—a sunny place! We let the place in Brattleboro go and bought Luce Hill."

Just before ending their first memorable Vermont summer, the family had an encounter with an authentic New Englander—slow to speak, firm of opinion, staunch and reliable. As Maria told it, "One day late in August a car stopped at our place and a very quiet gentleman got out. He introduced himself as Mr. Craig Burt of Stowe. And he didn't have too much to say. But I could see he wanted to ask me something. So I finally said, 'Where do you want us to sing, Mr. Burt?'"

"He was relieved, for that of course was what he wanted. 'The Army has taken over the CCC camp outside of Stowe, and they asked me to find entertainment for the boys, and so I thought of you people.' The next Saturday we were picked up in Army jeeps and taken to the CCC camp to sing. Then we agreed to sing a Mass for the soldiers the following Sunday."

The Trapps didn't realize it at the time, but they had been befriended by "The King of Stowe" when they met Craig Burt. This kindly, influential man became their "Uncle Craig," an important link in becoming Vermonters.

When the family returned to Merion and started the concert season, they had a new sense of belonging. After years of living in rented houses, riding the bus for endless miles, and constantly unpacking and packing in hotels, they had a home. The land of Luce Hill was fondly called "The Farm," despite its neglected, run-down condition. Since Vermont was dairy country, a plan emerged that between tours, the family would work together to establish a self-supporting home. Each person planned to pursue his or her own special interest on the farm.

The first project that needed attention was the enlargement of the old farmhouse to accommodate the large family. War restrictions forbade the construction of a new building, but did permit a remodeling project. In the early spring, a second story was planned and started. When the roof was lifted, a mountain blizzard blew most of the house into the cellar. Opening the door from the remaining two-room kitchen ell meant looking right into Vermont.

That summer, most of the family camped in tents and in the barn while the mess was cleared away, and the house was started again. A very creative architect living in Stowe designed a plan for a twenty-room, wide-roofed Tyrolean chalet, not unlike the Erlhof of Grandmother

of Whitehead in Zell-am-See.

With World War II creating labor shortages, the Trapp family pitched in to build their new home. They dug ditches, mixed cement, planted trees, mowed hay, and tended the fields and farmyard. They learned about the big dairy herd and raised pigs for their own table and to sell as pork.

With the help of a tenant farmer who looked after the farm when the Trapps were on tour, the family did most of the farm work.

The farm included its own sugar bush, and the first sap run in early

Top: Haying time on the Trapp Family Farm, with the Green Mountains in the distance. A series of photographs showing the family's busy life in the country appeared in Life Magazine *in November, 1943, adding to their fame in America. Above: The labor shortage prompted the Captain to remark to a visitor that "We could use a few more men on the place." The response was, "Yep. Or one more of those girls." Here, Johanna, the Captain, Agathe and Maria mix cement for the cellar and foundation. Left: Johannes pitched in to help on the family farm even as a young boy. He said his favorite days were spent in blue jeans, working and exploring the family acreage.*

spring meant tapping hundreds of maple trees. The family worked together at sugaring, thoroughly enjoying the work of collecting and boiling the sap. The sap was transformed into syrup in the sugar house and became a cash crop. "Sugar on snow" parties relieved the days of toil during the maple syrup season.

As Johannes said of their farming life, the family "got up early, went to Mass, had breakfast, went to work, and worked all day." Mass was held in a chicken coop converted into a chapel. "Was it not true that the Lord was born in a lowly barn?" the family replied to those who questioned their temporary chapel.

"Life for the Trapps took on a new meaning," said Maria von Trapp of their new home on the farm. "Coming from Austria, Vermont was the best state for us to settle in. Thank God for having led us to Vermont!"

Top left: Collecting sap from the maple woods was an annual ritual of early spring. Maple syrup from the sugar house was canned and sold as a cash crop.

Above: Martina applies labels to cans of Trapp Family syrup, while Maria and Eleonore use the fruit of the season in cooking.

Left: The family enjoyed sugar-on-snow parties during the maple sugar season.

Left: The first triumph in Vermont: the finished addition and remodeling job of the Austrian-style house. The small building in the foreground was used as a temporary dining hall during construction of the house. Later, Maria von Trapp used it as a writing studio.

Above: The entrance way was shaded by a massive poplar tree. Left: The bay window off the big living room became a favorite place to rehearse for concerts.

The heart of the new house was the living room, which opened onto a step-up library alcove.

The second floor chapel was a later addition to the original house.

Decorations by Agathe von Trapp

Chapter 9

Christmas with the Trapp Family Singers

For the Trapp family, the Christmas season began with their Advent wreath. Captain von Trapp hung the circular wreath of fir twigs from the living room ceiling, and with the lighting of the first of four candles, the holy season was ushered in. On the same day, each family member drew another's name from a bowl, and was responsible for supplying an anonymous surprise every day until Christmas. The Christmas manger scene was set up in the living room. Like most families, the Trapps prized their Christmas decorations, and cherished them from year to year.

The whole house teemed with preparations, both secret and visible. In the kitchen, the making of candies and cookies filled the air with tantalizing aromas. The creative Trapps made many of their own gifts for giving. On the morning of December 6, there was spicy *Lebkuchen*, marking the visit of St. Nicholas on his feast-day. The kindly saint made his call to learn, through letters left by the youngest family members, their fondest wishes for Christmas gifts. In Austria, Santa Claus did not leave presents; the Christ Child Himself came down from heaven to leave earthly evidences of His love.

On December 24, the living room was off-limits so that the Christmas tree could be prepared. It towered to the ceiling, decked with silver chains, cookies, candies, ornaments, and real wax candles. When they were lit, the tree and all of its gifts beneath were bathed in a warm glow.

"Then we read the Gospel of St. Luke, sang 'Silent Night,' and opened the presents," said Rupert. "We all went to bed early, to get some rest before Midnight Mass, and at eleven o'clock, my father would go around singing a certain song to wake us up, as if to the shepherds. It was 'Hirten, auf um Mitternacht.'" ("Shepherds Wake Up at Midnight.")

From door to door, the Captain roused his "shepherds," and each joined him with a lantern. When all assembled, they walked through the snow and cold to church. In Austria, the dark night was full of specks of lantern light as families came down the mountainsides to the village churches. At home in Vermont, the procession of Trapps assembled in

The Captain places the star atop the family tree.

Overleaf: The Trapp Family Lodge at Christmastime.

The pre-holiday concertizing was often the most strenuous of the whole year for the Trapps. Their Christmas concerts were booked heavily, and some cities asked for return visits each year. In 1946, they checked into their favorite New York hotel, the Wellington, to stay during their Town Hall appearances. A journalist found them there, and wrote of their busy lives in a feature titled "Salzburg in the Subway":

Looking as if they had just stepped off a Tyrolean Alp, Baron Georg von Trapp, Baroness Maria von Trapp, their seven daughters and two sons, and Dr. Franz Wasner, arrived in their own bus . . . After morning mass, said by Father Wasner . . . the family split up for the morning. The Baroness attended to bookings; Rosmarie, Eleonore and Johannes studied with a French-Canadian tutor. The older girls shopped at handicraft stores for the materials for the presents each Trapp makes for every other Trapp. Baron von Trapp bought supplies for the 20-room house he and his family built on a 600-acre farm in Vermont. When we got to their hotel at noon, the Trapps, pink-cheeked and bright-eyed, had all been up for hours. In one small room we found Rosmarie, Johanna, Hedwig and Agathe, all dressed alike, at work on various handmade gifts. Silver and gold tinsel angels were strewn across the bed. Agathe's linoleum blocks for Christmas cards were piled on a table. Hedwig was smocking a blue cotton nightdress for her mother. On the floor sat Johannes, wearing a green-trimmed suit exactly like his father's and brothers', knitting a length of blue rope into bedroom slippers for his mother. In the next room Werner was forging handmade silver medallions and chains. Rupert was expected late that evening from the University of Vermont where he is in his last year of medical school.

"Please come in and don't get scared of the mess; I know it's terrible," said Hedwig, sweeping a partly finished hand-fringed scarf off a chair.

"Gosh darn it," Johannes mumbled, as he nearly dropped a stitch.

"Johannes!" reproached his sisters in unison.

"I wish I could have Werner's blow torch. I was going to melt the tinsel down and make something of it. We're very busy now. It's close to Christmas and we don't have much time in New York for school," Johannes said, his Yankee twang contrasting sharply with his sisters' soft, German accents.

Johannes, quite unself-conscious in his first press interview, said he was anxious to leave New York and get on to his favorite stop of every concert tour, Texas. "I like Texas best," he said, "because it's nice and hot and flat. No Agathe, it's not only the cowboys. You can ride better there and you don't have to duck for the trees."

Maria, who sings second soprano, plays the tenor recorder and viola da gamba, came in to tell us that her parents were waiting for us to join them for lunch downstairs.

In the hotel dining room, the Baroness Maria von Trapp, a tall, strong blue-eyed woman in radiant health, dressed like her daughters, and like them, without make-up, firmly pressed our hand, and then introduced us to the Baron, a twinkling-eyed man who looked like Santa Claus with a mustache instead of a beard. After ordering lunch, three full courses and double desserts, the Baroness apologized for the somewhat disordered state of the family's belongings, "but we're living on the bus and I'm stumbling over everything," she said.

After lunch, she and her family were going downtown to the headquarters of CARE (Co-operative for American Remittances to Europe) to send more food packages to Austria, the Baroness told us. They had already sent 120 packages, and when the family pig was slaughtered this fall, "we devoted her fat sides to Austria."

*Top: The Captain lights the Advent wreath.
Below: The Trapp Family recorded many
Christmas songs from their concerts.*

family members joined him, each with lanterns. In the early years, Johannes' lantern barely cleared the floor. With the glowing tree behind them, the Trapp Family Singers sat in the gentle lantern light, singing Christmas carols. Their repertoire included songs from Austria, Germany, Italy, Sweden, England, Mexico, Poland, Spain, and America.

Maria von Trapp related the folkways of Christmas in her family's homeland, and contributed a song that became almost a trademark for her. It was "The Virgin's Lullabye." Slowly and meditatively, she sang in her warm alto, with the family humming in the background.

Maria explained that encores would be sung within the concert, so that the high point, the most important song, would be the final selection. It was "Stille Nacht," "Silent Night." Maria explained that through her mother's family, she was related to the Rainer family, singers from the Zillertal, who toured Europe and America in the 1840s. They first brought "Silent Night" to the world, and the Trapp family continued the process. Standing in front of the lighted tree, the family sang a verse in German, then one in English, and while humming the melody, they quietly filed offstage. A tender silence filled the concert hall, with the peace of "Silent Night" hanging in the air.

One listener remarked, "I never heard 'Silent Night' until I heard the Trapp family sing it." First Lady Eleanor Roosevelt

their chapel for Mass.

In America, the Trapp Family simply transferred their Christmas customs and music from home to the concert stage. In 1940, the family performed the first of their beloved Christmas concerts. The overwhelming response made the holiday performance an annual tradition, and from late November until just before Christmas, the Trapps recreated the typical Austrian Holy Night on stages all over America.

Concertgoers saw the tall decorated tree, with a long table and chairs nearby. Stage lights would dim, and there was an expectant hush of anticipation. Father Wasner's deep bass began "Hirten auf..." One by one, the echoed these sentiments. When the Trapp family sang at the White House in December 1940, Mrs. Roosevelt mentioned their visit in her popular newspaper column, "My Day." "I don't think I ever heard 'Silent Night' more beautifully sung," she remarked.

In person, on radio, in movie newsreels, and on records, the Trapp Family Singers lovingly sang their Christmas music. An indefinable magic always accompanied them. Music critics commented on this quality. "Love of family, love of music, love of God, and longing for peace and good will combined so powerfully in the music offerings of this family that they transferred their emotion to the audience," wrote the *Washington Post*. "At the concert's climax, there was hardly a dry eye in the hall."

What did the sophisticated concertgoers in New York's Town Hall, Washington's Constitution Hall, and Boston's Jordan Hall find in the Christmas programs? One admirer tried to express these feelings. "Each new year finds us eager to hear again the Trapp Family Singers at Christmastide. They are an essential part of our Christmas. There is something inexplicably tender and moving within us as they sing their carols as we have never heard them sung before. I can only believe that the beautiful spirit of this family teaches us beyond the footlights. We go forth into a very different world with

their deep feeling of reverence . . ."

"People left our Christmas concerts with a real feeling of holiness," Eleonore declared. "They would come backstage and say, 'Thank you; you have just given me my Christmas.' And we just knew that God was at work through our concerts."

The Captain and Eleonore prepare the lanterns used in Christmas concerts. Below: The family's Christmas performances were annual treats in many American cities.

Chapter 10

Wartime Choir and Sing Weeks

America's involvement in World War II called upon the services of millions of sons and brothers, and the Trapp family was no exception in this sacrifice. Rupert and Werner left the family circle in 1943 to serve in the United States Army. Both boys entered the 10th Mountain Division as ski troopers.

Not only were Rupert and Werner sorely missed within the tightly knit family circle, their absent voices forced a reorganization of the Trapp Family Singers. Without Rupert's bass and Werner's tenor, the group became a woman's choir except for Father Wasner's bass. Father Wasner speedily rewrote his choral arrangements, and audiences accepted what Maria von Trapp called "the war edition of the Trapp Family Singers." After all, many families had sons away at war and had to endure without them.

It was at this time that Rosmarie and Eleonore joined the family choir on a regular basis. For several years they had studied recorder, and they made their debut at Town Hall in 1941. "When my brothers were drafted, I knew that I could help fill a gap," said Eleonore. "I never questioned this, and I knew that there was a sense of mission connected with our singing, something more than earning a living."

War imposed restrictions on gasoline use, so tours were necessarily made by train. Each day was a challenge, dealing with luggage, finding space on trains filled with the military, and managing for everyone to arrive at the next concert destination on time. In Kansas, a train to Wichita was canceled, and the local concert manager could produce only a hearse as transportation. The family sang and yodeled all the way, causing intense curiosity among the people they passed who had never seen a singing hearse. When they arrived in Wichita, people gaped again when the hearse unloaded the dirndl-clad Trapps.

While the family had its adventures on the road, Rupert and Werner endured the rigors of Army life at Camp Hale, Colorado. "First

Rupert and Werner with their stepmother during World War II.

Facing page, upper left: Under the Trapp Family Music Camp sign. Below: Father Wasner conducts the camp choir under the trees. Lower right: Music camp guest roster.

Top: Eleonore and Rosmarie playing recorders. Right: Father Wasner rehearses with the Trapp Family Singers in Stowe, 1943. Above: Martina (left) and Johanna practice recorder music, 1943.

we trained endlessly and then we were sent to Texas to stand by for Europe, 14,000 men and 9,000 mules," Rupert recalled. "For the first time in my life, I was me," he said, referring to the new role he held in active fighting against Nazism. The 10th Mountain Division eventually served in the Italian Appenines. There Rupert was a medical orderly, because his Austrian medical degree was not recognized by the American Army. But often, his colonel consulted him on medical advice.

The boys missed the experience of rebuilding the family's American home on Luce Hill in Stowe, but learned of its progress through letters. Few people in Stowe knew that the Trapp sons were fighting the war in Europe, and some viewed the Trapps' presence with suspicion. Why were those German-speaking people in town? And what were they constructing high atop Luce Hill?

The brief interlude of mistrust ended one memorable evening near summer's end in 1943. News of the Trapp Family's huge success in outdoor summer concerts at Meridian Hill Park in Washington, D.C. was reported by the media. This gave some Stowe village leaders an idea. "High school officials approached us one day with a request," Agathe recalled. "Would we give a concert for the benefit of the school? A new roof was needed and there was not enough money for this project. We agreed."

Eleonore remembered, "We didn't have any money to contribute with all of our own building expenses on the farm, so we decided to give this benefit concert just for the Stowe people. Afterwards, the five selectmen stood up, and one of them said he wanted to welcome us in the name of the people of Stowe. Then, the whole audience lined up to shake hands with us. That was the Vermonters' way of saying, 'We accept you.'"

Shortly thereafter, the Trapps experienced their first Vermont roof raising. Carpentry students swarmed over their unfinished house, so that the family could leave on concert tour with a snug home to return to. "They were like gnomes all over the place," marveled Maria von Trapp. "It was like something from a fairy tale!"

Soon after the family settled

in Stowe, Maria realized that their farm was simply too beautiful to keep to themselves; they had to share the place with others. At first, there was no way to accommodate all the people who wished to visit the Trapp Family Singers in their home. But during one Christmas interim between tours, they discovered the abandoned CCC (Civilian Conservation Corps) camp at the foot of their hill. An idea emerged: Why not have Sing Weeks there?

So many people came backstage after concerts, or wrote letters asking, "How can I get my family to sing?" that a music camp directed by the Trapps seemed a perfect answer. Previously, Maria

Above: Like other American families during the war, the Trapps waited for mail and news from their sons and brothers who were overseas fighting. Below: Maria (left) rehearses with Mother and Johanna.

Above: An Easter concert at New York's Town Hall in 1945. Left: A staged publicity shot before a concert in Chicago in 1945 shows the non-singing Captain leading the choir in song. From left: Mother, Georg, Eleonore, Johannes, Agathe, Hedwig, Rosmarie, Martina, Johanna, and Maria.

ken-down conditions in postwar Austria, and asked if the Trapp Family could help their homeland through the powerful medium of their concertizing.

The response was immediate and heartwarming. At most concerts, and in radio and press interviews, Maria von Trapp gave what the family called "Mother's Austrian Relief Speech." Generous Americans responded, bringing clothing, foodstuffs, and supplies of all kinds to the bus, to be shipped to Austria. During the long drives, the Trapps worked as a one-family relief organization, systematically packing and preparing the needed goods for Austria.

For many of the neediest Austrians, the work of Trapp Family Austrian Relief spelled the difference between life and death. Army chaplains in Salzburg and Vienna distributed the supplies to deserving citizens. Heart-rending letters came back across the ocean, full of appreciation. Through its years of existence, the family's relief organization shipped over 275,000 pounds of material to Austria. But this feat was not stressed by the family members; they preferred to be mindful of Christ's exhortation in regards to charity: "So when you give to the needy, do not announce it with trumpets . . . " (Matthew 6:2).

Throughout the spring 1947 concert tour to the West Coast and the busy collecting for Austrian Relief, Captain von Trapp steadfastly accompanied his family, but often he wearily retired to the cot in the rear of the bus. He hid his fatigue and a persistent cough from the family until he flew from Seattle to New York City, where he had faith in a doctor who had treated him earlier.

Above Left: Rehearsing for tour in Stowe.

Above Right: Rupert with Austrian Relief packages.

Above: The Captain and Werner prepare a shipment for Austrian Relief.

Top: The last family portrait of the Trapps, at home in Stowe, 1946. Front: Eleonore, Agathe, Johanna, Mother, Johannes, Georg, and Rosmarie. Back: Werner, Martina, Rupert, Hedwig, and Maria.

Above: Georg and Maria at home in Stowe.

The family kept to its performing schedule, but health reports finally convinced Maria that she should join her husband in New York.

Captain von Trapp's health had greatly deteriorated; he was suffering from an undiagnosed lung cancer. His wife took him home to Stowe for rest and recuperation, and they awaited the family's return from the concert trip. There was a brief reunion, and the loving Papa delighted in learning about the last concerts, the Austrian relief work, and each individual family member's news and concerns. As always he was selfless and quietly heroic. In case he did not recover, he urged: "Please don't bury me with shoes—send them to the needy in Europe." Should he die, the Captain asked that there be no great unhappiness; instead, he said, "Thank God that I have reached my goal."

The end came for Georg von Trapp during the night of May 30, 1947. He died at home with his family surrounding him.

In their grief, the Captain's family honored his last wishes. They sang over his body in the flower-filled living room, while a gravesite was prepared just a few hundred feet from the house. On the burial day, a cross bearer led the procession, and the family sang one of their father's favorite lullabies. Eight friends bore the coffin, which was covered with a flag from his submarine. An

"The bishop gave us permission to have our own little cemetery near our house, and from there, the Captain is still running the ship," said Maria of her husband's gravesite.

Left: Captain Georg von Trapp.

Austrian custom was carried out at the gravesite: each family member and mourner sprinkled holy water and dirt into the grave.

Georg von Trapp had lived the life of an extraordinary man. As his daughter Agathe observed, "He was a hero in warfare and a hero in his everyday living . . . a quiet man, but when he spoke, one listened. He lived his life upright, without complaining, always finding things to do which were helpful to his family."

Despite their loss, the Trapp Family carried on. The farm, the summer music camp, the collections for Austria . . . these activities filled the summer of 1947. There were other family illnesses that year to contend with, including a near-fatal one for the newly widowed Maria. The children sang on the fall concert tour without either parent, and Christmas concerts were performed while Maria lay between life and death in a hospital.

Of these dark months, Maria said later, "There are times when you don't have to search for the Will of God. You have to keep still . . . your whole being says, 'Thy Will be done.' While you are sad down to the core of your being, you are also at peace."

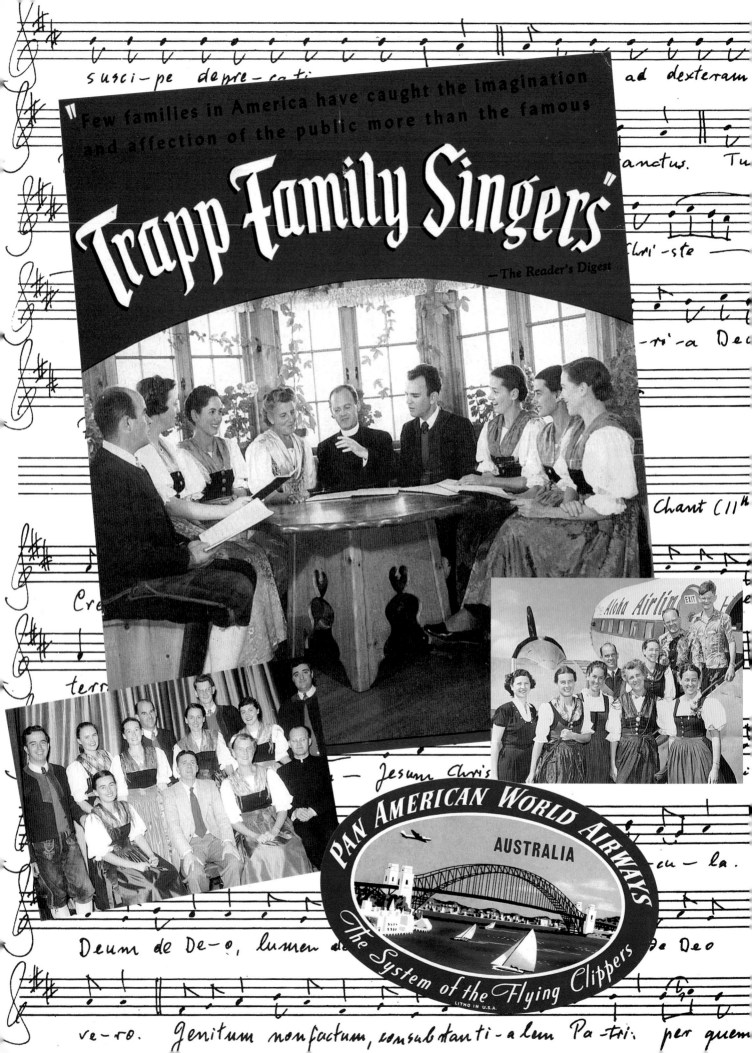

Chapter 12

On Wings and Wheels

Following Captain von Trapp's death, there were many changes within the family circle, both personally and professionally. Rupert completed his M.D. degree just before his father died, and later that year he married Henriette Lajoie, a member of a family who became acquainted with the Trapps at the Music Camp. Rupert spent two years in hospital training before starting his own family practice in Little Compton, Rhode Island.

On Easter Monday, 1948, Johanna married Ernst Florian Winter, who had known Rupert and Werner during their war service. The Winter family shared experiences with the Trapps; they too were Austrian refugees from the Nazis. In America Ernst earned his Ph.D. and began a career as a professor and diplomat.

Soon after Christmas 1948, Werner married Erika Klambauer in the chapel at home. Erika was a school friend of Martina's, who had weathered the war years near Salzburg. During a postwar visit to Stowe, Erika and Werner were engaged. After a Canadian honeymoon, Werner was able to show his bride more of America when she joined the family on a concert tour.

In 1949, Martina and Jean Dupire were married inStowe. Martina's French Canadian husband had become acquainted with the family through the Music Camp, and a romance developed. Martina continued to sing with the family after marriage, as did Werner.

Family developments meant reorganizing the singing group. Rupert and Johanna left the group permanently, and Rosmarie, who said she always suffered from stage fright, no longer toured. For two seasons, a tenor named Donald Meissner was hired to sing with the family. Johannes developed a fine boy soprano voice to contribute to the choir, as well as an expertise on the recorder.

There were changes at home as well as on stage. Operating the farm with absentee management had never been efficient, so the dairy herd was sold. Another more productive crop sprung up in Stowe: the skiers. Stowe was dubbed "Ski Capital of the East," and the winter visitors needed lodging. When the family was on tour, their empty rooms were rented out, and the family cook provided meals.

During the summer months, rooms were also available while the family lived at the Music Camp. Overflow guests and non-musical relatives of campers were accommodated at the house. One camp rule was inviolate: non-participants could not occupy space at the camp itself.

In 1948, an order of missionaries offered to purchase the Trapp villa in Aigen. Its ownership had reverted back to the family, and when

Rupert and Henriette's wedding, 1947.

Werner and Erika's wedding, 1948.

Martina and Jean Dupire's wedding. Facing page, left inset: With Jack the bus driver in New Zealand. Right inset: The family arrives in Hawaii for their first visit in 1952.

111

*Rehearsal in the bay window of the house.
Facing page: The Cathedral in Salzburg, where
the Trapps gave an open-air concert.*

Designed by Agathe von Trapp

they sold the place it became known as St. Joseph's Seminary. With the money, debts were paid on the property in Stowe, and two guest wings were added to the house. Now, when Maria von Trapp announced from the stage, "Come see us in Stowe, Vermont," there was actually enough room to entertain the visitors.

When the family sought a name for their home, they settled on "Cor Unum," meaning "one heart." The name fit. It described the lives of the early Christians who lived cooperatively, each sharing with the group. Family life among the Trapps mirrored that example.

On an auspicious day in May 1948, members of Cor Unum drove to Montpelier, Vermont to be sworn in as American citizens. Along with natives of a half-dozen other countries, the Trapp Family repeated the oath of allegiance. They dropped "von" from their names and became simply "Trapps."

With a decade of adventures in America behind the family, Maria Trapp decided to write a book about their lives. Her introduction to the publishing world developed before the Captain's death, during a performance in Philadelphia. When an essential piece of luggage was discovered missing just before curtain time, the Captain hurried to retrieve it at the hotel. To stall for time, Maria stood on the empty stage regaling the audience with tales of life on tour. When she heard her husband's distinctive cough—a signal from backstage—she knew that all was well, and the concert proceeded.

In the audience was Bert Lippincott of the J. B. Lippincott Publishing Company. He stormed backstage with the theory that anyone who could tell stories so eloquently could also write a book. That encouragement led to *The Story of the Trapp Family Singers*, published in 1949. Maria dictated the book in six weeks, weaving the life of the family into an exciting and romantic tale. In her usual voluble way, she exceeded the suggested length by 50,000 words, which she cheerfully cut and saved for a sequel.

The Story of the Trapp Family Singers was widely read, and in 1950 it was awarded the Catholic Writers Guild's honor for the best book of nonfiction. The book has never gone out of print, selling over a million copies in many languages.

In April, May, and June of 1950, the Trapp Family Singers

The return to Salzburg was a memorable experience, including three performances at the time of the Salzburg Festival.

The baroque Collegiate Church in Salzburg.

concertized in South America. They took their music to stages in Mexico, Guatemala, and Panama; they sang their way through the Caribbean Islands and Venezuela. Then they went on to Brazil and Argentina. They flew across the Andes for concerts in Chile, Ecuador, Peru, and Colombia. The South American audiences were warmly appreciative. Werner recalled, "Rio de Janeiro was great; we had eleven curtain calls!" One enthused backstage admirer searched for the perfect compliment. "You biggest mother in world!" he finally told Maria Trapp.

Eleonore, who turned nineteen on the tour, remembered the excitement of frequent flights, visits to the jungle, and the thrill of performing in Argentina. The Teatro Colon in Buenos Aires was a duplicate of La Scala in Milan. "It was so special to sing there," she said, "because our voices just floated automatically with the perfect acoustics. Backstage, after our second concert, the Austrian conductor of 'The Magic Flute' came up to Father Wasner and said, 'I hope you

know what you have in this choir; it is like one instrument.'"

South America offered Father Wasner new music to arrange for the choir, and he wrote settings for folk songs from Brazil, Chile, and Argentina. He filled fifteen pounds of manuscript paper with Latin American music.

Johannes, at eleven, was a budding naturalist. He pressed examples of South American flora and fauna between pages of books and acquired a Peruvian ostrich egg. In Panama City his prize was an eight-inch scorpion which he preserved in a bottle of cologne. These eclectic treasures were among the family's luggage when they returned to the United States following their tour.

There was just time to conduct sessions of the Music Camp before the Trapps sailed to Europe for a concert tour in August 1950. Because of their continuing Austrian Relief work, the Trapp Family was given a heroic welcome when they arrived in Salzburg. It had been arranged that they lodge at their former home in Aigen, and while there, the family salvaged what they could of belongings remaining in the house. Important items were shipped to Stowe, and the rest were auctioned.

The Trapp Family Singers performed three times during the Salzburg Festival before continuing on to sing in nine more countries. They performed in Italy, Germany, Belgium, France, Sweden, Denmark, Norway, Wales, and England. By December they were back in America for their usual Christmas concerts. The busy year of travel ended with a live radio broadcast of holiday music from New York on Christmas Eve.

When the family departed for a tour of the West Coast in January 1951, Martina remained behind at Cor Unum. She and her husband Jean were expecting their first child, so they busied themselves at home in anticipation of the event. Martina wrote the family, "I thank you all for being so nice about me staying home," but she also missed the concert work. She followed the family's itinerary, and waited for letters and news of the tour. When she learned that Werner's little Barbara was on stage, she exclaimed, "That must have been cute! Oh, I can imagine it so well . . ."

After a concert in late February, Maria received shocking news from home. As she related, "The telephone rang and a voice on the other end said, 'Mother, Martina is dead.'" She had died in childbirth, along with her daughter Notburga. The family sang a requiem in a California church for their sister, and despite the tragedy, continued the tour. Martina was buried near her father in the little cemetery behind the house.

The loss of Martina made another permanent absence in the family choir, and when Johannes' voice changed, two "non-Trapps" were recruited at the Music Camp to fill the gaps. They were a young couple, Hal and Charlene Peterson. As Maria explained:

"One afternoon Father Wasner said, 'Wouldn't it be wonderful if we had people like this in our group?' 'Well, why not ask them,' I said, and I still remember the place where I stopped Charlene and asked her if they could join the Trapp Family Singers for the season. 'But I don't think we are good enough,' she said . . . The truth is that they are both very, very good musicians and have enhanced our concert group ever since."

The Petersons sang with the family on their second tour of the Hawaiian islands, and when they returned to California the group stopped for two days with Bob and Dolores Hope. They attended Bob's fiftieth birthday party, and as Hal Peterson recalled, "Char and I just stood around and stared, for there were radio and movie stars all over the place. Later in the evening we sang a few songs, and a little impromptu show was put on. It was really a wonderful evening."

In June 1954, Eleonore's wedding to Hugh Campbell was celebrated at Cor Unum. Although Eleonore had felt a sense of mission singing with the family, she also felt a calling to become a wife and mother. The loss of her soprano in the choir was keenly felt. She was replaced by Barbara Stechow of Oberlin, Ohio.

Early in 1955 an announcement was mailed out, saying "There will be NO Trapp Family

Martina's grave. Below: Eleonore and Hugh Campbell's wedding at the Music Camp chapel.

(Photo courtesy of Barbara S. Harris)

Rehearsing with Father Wasner at Cor Unum for the Australian-New Zealand tour, 1955. From left: Father Wasner, Peter La Manna, Barbara Stechow, Johannes, Annette Brophy, Hedwig, Mother, Maria, Werner, Agathe, and Alvaro Villa.

Maria, Mother and Johannes on an Australian magazine cover.

Music Camp this summer because—WE GO TO AUS-TRALIA AND NEW ZEALAND!" Rehearsals for the tour began at Cor Unum in March, and included three additional singers: Annette Brophy of Utah, Alvaro Villa of Colombia, and Peter La Manna of Pennsylvania. Along with Father Wasner, Mother Trapp, Agathe, Maria, Hedwig, Barbara Stechow, Werner and Johannes, this group became the final version of the Trapp Family Singers.

In her stage introductions, Mother Trapp humorously explained the presence of new members of the singing group: "We are the von Trapps; they are the non-Trapps!" Annette Brophy, a Juilliard-trained soprano, recalled that singing with the family "affected my whole life . . . I was with people I loved, singing wonderful music. And Father Wasner taught me so much, all in this warm environment."

The New Zealand-Australia tour was, as Johannes said, "our longest and most exciting tour." It spanned six months, from May-October, and included 230 concerts. From the time the family disembarked the plane in Auckland, New Zealand, they were a sensation; entertainers from abroad were a rarity at that time. Warm welcomes and enthusiasm for their work followed the group through their 29-city tour of the North and South Islands.

Barbara Stechow, who turned eighteen on the tour, wrote her family of the outstanding reception: "The concert-goers have a wonderful custom . . . they wait after a concert outside the theater doors, and give a last 'three cheers' for the artists. We always feel really appreciated. Almost every night in Christchurch this custom caused a traffic jam, with people crowding all around our bus to hear our last encore, usually 'Brahms Lullabye' . . ."

New Zealand offered the Trapp Family a chance to explore native culture and folkways when they visited a Maori *pa*. They heard the native chants and songs, and discovered the intricate poi dance. The poi dance found its way into Trapp Family concerts, as well as Maori melodies with arrangements by Father Wasner. He also created a stirring arrangement of "Waltzing Matilda" in anticipation of the Australian concerts.

The tour of Australia took the Trapp Family Singers to the outback for a tour of small towns, as well as to the grandest theaters in Melbourne, Brisbane, Adelaide, and Sydney. They experienced the aboriginal culture and saw kangaroo, koala, and wallaby. They performed for thousands of schoolchildren, and even recreated their

Christmas concert in Melbourne's Town Hall.

During the New Zealand-Australia concert tour, the family realized, as Mother Trapp said, "It was time to say *auf Wiedersehen* to our melodies together, but never to the wonder of our memories and fine music."

Learning about the Maori culture with a native guide (center) at Rotorua, New Zealand.

"We sing with the Maoris."

En route to New Zealand, the group stopped for concerts in Hawaii. (Photo courtesy of Annette B. Jacobs.)

117

The Trapp Family Lodge became one of Stowe's major attractions. Flowers, good food, and magnificent views made the inn a legendary vacation spot.

Trapp
Family
Lodge

Chapter 13

New Directions for the Trapp Family

"Twenty years is a long time to stand on the stage and sing," Werner observed. Each family member sacrificed personal goals to keep the singing group intact for so many seasons; no choral group in history had kept the same voices for so long. "It had lasted long, and turned out unbelievably well, but it was time to lead quieter lives," Father Wasner remarked of the decision to disband the Trapp Family Singers.

Before the family bowed out of public life, they made a Farewell Tour in December 1955 and January 1956. A critic wrote after one of the final concerts, "When Father Wasner said good-by, we were sad to see it end. His reply voiced the feeling of all the Trapps: 'We hope it does not end. We hope that what we have done will carry on . . . out into the world.'"

The family who sang together simply because they loved singing had shared their music with millions of listeners in over 2,000 concerts throughout thirty countries.

The Music Camp was discontinued after the summer sessions in 1956. By the end of the year, some of the family members accepted an invitation from the apostolic delegate of Sydney, Australia to "come back and do something for the missions." Maria, Rosmarie, and Johannes headed to the jungles of New Guinea to labor as lay missionaries 10,000 miles from home. Their mother, along with Father Wasner, toured the South Seas on a fact-finding mission.

Maria, Rosmarie, and Johannes were stationed on New Guinea's Fergusson Island. Johannes built a school from timber dragged through the water from nearby islands, and assisted local men in the construction of a church. The girls taught English to native children, but their first link with them was through music. Maria recalled, "We had two choirs and sang songs we had used in our concerts! We taught music and folk dancing, and adapted native melodies to sacred words."

Mother Trapp was deeply impressed with the importance of mission work in the South Seas, and hoped that lay missionaries would flood the islands. She said, "Christianity is starting from scratch there; it's not enough to send money to the natives. Nurses, teachers, doctors, priests,

Leaving for New Guinea for the first time, 1956. Left to Right: Rosmarie, Mother Trapp, Johannes, Maria, and Father Wasner.

anyone . . . they are needed to live with the natives, treat them as equals, pitch in, and help."

With the "Flying Bishop," Most Reverend Leo Arckfeld, Mother Trapp and Father Wasner saw incredible sights as they journeyed by plane and boat. Mother Trapp was sometimes the first white woman the headhunters and cannibals had seen. "When we arrived," she said, "one village had just eaten another. A ring of these natives confronted me just when I realized my nylons were twisted around my leg. I stooped over to straighten them, when with one voice they uttered a frightening grunt. I was frightened, but the chief politely asked me to do it again. Do *what* again? Straighten your skin!"

After twenty-four years with the Trapp Family, Father Wasner volunteered for missionary work in the Fiji Islands. He was installed at the mission station of Naiserelangi. Father Wasner did outstanding work in building up the rundown mission which overlooked Viti Levu Bay and several picturesque Fijian villages. He made visitations on horseback, and developed strong interest in recording and preserving Fijian art, music, and customs.

Johannes and Rosmarie con-

Erika von Trapp in the Lodge gardens.

Daughter Maria in New Guinea with a small Papuan friend.

tinued to work with their sister Maria in New Guinea for several years before returning home. Maria made her work in New Guinea a lifetime vocation. "She eats, drinks, and breathes Mission," Mother Trapp noted when Maria finally took home leave in 1961. "She hasn't changed a bit—the same twinkle in her eyes and the same infectious 'Mitzi-laugh', those ringing scales of laughter, so irresistible that you have to join in."

After the singing years, the Trapp Family was scattered widely. Rupert and Eleonore settled in southern New England. Rupert's family included six children, and Eleonore's consisted of seven daughters. Johanna returned to Austria with her husband and seven children.

Agathe and Hedwig both leaned toward teaching professions. With her friend, Mary Lou Kane, Agathe opened a kindergarten in Stowe. Later, they moved to Glyndon, Maryland and founded Sacred Heart Kindergarten. Hedwig assisted in keeping Cor Unum open for guests, but in 1960 she began working with a Catholic youth organization in Honolulu. She started a choir, taught handicrafts, cooking, and carpentry, and was a dynamic force among the children. As an adult, one of Hedwig's students declared, "She was the most inspiring teacher I ever had."

Werner also tackled teaching at a music school in Pennsylvania, but in 1959 he bought a dairy farm near the

Above: Maria and Hedwig on the Lodge porch.
Left: Hedwig in the Lodge gardens. Below: The
Lodge in the spring.

Above: Agathe carved the likeness of the Blessed Mother over the altar.

Left: "Our Lady of Peace" chapel, built by Werner at the Lodge.

The Lodge became a favorite hostelry for skiers.

Above: Maria enjoyed meeting Lodge guests. Here she joins a group for coffee in the bay window.
Left: Breakfast with Hedwig, Mother, and Johannes in the South Pacific Room of the Lodge.

Vermont village of Waitsfield. His wife Erika shared Werner's love of agriculture, and their children actively helped on the family farm. "Fortunately it is only forty minutes from Stowe," Mother Trapp said, "so I rush over every so often. Erika always keeps fresh buttermilk for me, and there is no better rye bread than hers."

Eleonore and her husband Hugh purchased land from Werner for a house, so the Trapp Family presence in the Waitsfield vicinity was well established.

Except for gatherings and reunions, the only family member regularly in residence at Cor Unum was mother and grandmother, Maria. The house became the Trapp Family Lodge, a famous New England inn of great charm. Guests enjoyed the mountain views, the Austrian cookery, and quiet atmosphere. Maria was a genial hostess, and she thrived on interactions with the visitors. Her appearance at dinnertime to mingle with guests was a lodge tradition. Always wearing her colorful Austrian dirndl, she served coffee in the bay window, told stories, and encouraged folk dancing and lively discussions.

Maria also presided over the Trapp Family Gift Shop. This was her pet project, founded despite "the cold eye" she said the family gave her. "I don't have a head for business, and they were sure it wouldn't work," she remarked. The shop specialized in Trapp Family books and records, and crafts from around the world. Buying for the shop took Maria to

Europe twice a year, with stops in Austria. The shop occupied a separate building near the Lodge, which was expanded to include Vermont's first Viennese-style coffeehouse.

Johannes assisted at the Lodge during vacations from Dartmouth College, and later from Yale Forestry School. He had appreciated the natural beauty of the family property since his boyhood, and contributed many workable ideas to enhance the resort. For winter guests who wanted alternatives to the downhill slopes of nearby Mount Mansfield, Johannes introduced cross-country skiing. Trails were cut through the woods behind the Lodge, and rental equipment was first issued from a garage. From this modest start, sixty miles of pristine trails developed. The Trapp Family Cross-Country Ski Touring Center became North America's first commercial establishment devoted to Nordic skiing.

Johannes converted his accident-prone mother to the bucolic pleasures of ski-touring in the snowy woods and meadows. When she was home, she skied across the trails nearly every winter day. "Thank God for cross-country skiing," Maria exclaimed.

During the years after the concertizing ended, Maria was often on the road, traveling as a lecturer. Billed as Baroness Maria von Trapp, she crossed the country many times, telling the story of her family. She always assured her audiences, "If God can do so much for the Trapp Family, He can do the same for you."

Left: Flowers have always been a Trapp Family trademark at the Lodge. Above: The foliage season at Lodge is a favorite time for visitors. Below: The Lodge in winter, showing the rock garden.

(Photo: E.L. Sheldon)

Chapter 14

A New Song:
The Sound of Music

The German film company, Gloria, produced two movies based on *The Story of the Trapp Family Singers* in the late 1950s. The films, *The Trapp Family* and *The Trapp Family in America*, were well received throughout the world; in Munich the first movie ran for 24 weeks and in Tokyo for 34 weeks. When Broadway actress Mary Martin saw the film, she said, "I knew it was for me." An adaptation of the Trapp Family story was envisioned as a musical play, with Mary Martin in the role of Maria.

The real Maria was deep in the tropics on her tour of the mission stations when the first flickers of interest were shown in adapting her book for the stage. Since the musical version was intended as a vehicle for Mary Martin, Maria was invited to see the actress perform in *Annie Get Your Gun* in San Francisco. The two developed an excellent rapport, but Maria still shied away from an adaptation.

Finally, producer Leland Hayward followed Maria to Europe, where she was recovering from the malaria she acquired in the South Seas. He pointed out that royalties would aid the mission work she supported, and Maria agreed. The musical became *The Sound of Music*.

Before rehearsals started in 1959, Mary Martin arrived at the Trapp Family Lodge to prepare for her role. "For two blessed weeks, she studied me!" Maria said. "I'm famous for taking very unladylike, long steps and talking with my hands. In walking around the house, I always saw Mary out of the corner of my eye, imitating me." Maria also taught Mary how to folk dance, how to kneel, to cross herself, and play the guitar.

"And I taught her a Texas yodel," Mary Martin recalled. "We decided that I was born in Texas, and she was born in Austria, but underneath we were the same Maria."

The Sound of Music opened in New York on November 16, 1959, and depicted Maria's arrival in the von Trapp home, her marriage to the Captain, and the family's escape from Austria. Theodore Bikel portrayed

Ruth Leuwerik **Die Trapp-Familie** *in Amerika* GLORIA
Ein Divina-Farbfilm der Gloria

Above: The Gloria film cast which depicted the Trapp Family Singers. Facing page: Julie Andrews as Maria in The Sound of Music. *(Photo: Photo Fest)*

Maria and Mary Martin at the Trapp Family Lodge, August, 1959. "One of the joys of my life was portraying Maria," said Mary. (Photo: Photo Fest)

Mary Martin onstage with the Broadway version of the Trapp Family. Photo: Billy Rose Collection, New York; Public Library for the Performing Arts.

the Captain. "I had not been warned that he would make his entrance in his captain's uniform," Maria noted. "When he came on, it took my breath away. Seeing Mary Martin as me made me feel funny—sort of awkward.

"All of the important things were true," Maria said of the compacted version of the Trapp history. Among the minor changes was the renaming of the seven children. Rodgers and Hammerstein's music for the play achieved classic status with such songs as "Climb

Ev'ry Mountain," "Do-Re-Mi," "My Favorite Things," and "The Sound of Music."

The musical ran for three years on Broadway. Its message of hope, patriotism, and family strength had universal appeal for audiences of all ages. "What a role, what a show, what a joy to millions and millions of people all over the world!" Mary Martin exclaimed.

Soon after *The Sound of Music* premiered came a surprise. Maria said, "Like a thunderbolt one day came the invitation that the Trapp Family Singers should bring out a record of *The Sound of Music*. After much hesitation we finally got seven members of the old group together, hired the Juilliard String Quartet and a few additional voices, and made the Warner Brothers record . . . *Hi Fi Magazine* mentions 'the excellent arrangements and the skillful direction of Franz Wasner' and finally calls it 'the finest and most artistic presentation of the score now to be found on records.'"

The Sound of Music was scheduled to become a Twentieth Century Fox movie, a fact that caused some concern for Maria. "For heaven's sake, what am I going to do if they have me twice divorced in this film?" she worried. Eleonore sympathized with her mother. "We were leery of this news," she said. "We wondered what Hollywood would do with our family of seven daughters!"

Maria had a chance to see the filming of *The Sound of Music* firsthand when she happened to visit Salzburg with family members in 1964. She shook hands with Julie Andrews, who portrayed her, and met Christopher Plummer, who played the Captain. And Maria fulfilled a lifelong wish: she appeared in a movie. During the filming of Julie Andrews' song "I Have Confidence," Maria, Rosmarie, and granddaughter Barbara were instructed to amble across the background. The short scene was repeated nineteen times, so Maria decided, "Right there and then I knew I have no

talent to be a film actress!"

The Sound of Music was an incredible success when it was released in 1965, and it catapulted the Trapp Family into a renown they had never sought nor expected. But family members were little affected by the movie. When Rupert attended the opening, he paid for his own tickets. He thought the movie was "all wet,"

On a visit to Salzburg in 1964, Maria discovered that The Sound of Music *was being filmed. Here, she shakes hands with Christopher Plummer (the Captain in the movie version). Also seen is Robert Wise, producer. Photo: Photo Fest.*

Above: The Sound of Music's *von Trapp Family. (Photo: Photo Fest)*

since he was portrayed as the eldest daughter. When asked who he was in the film, he affected a mock curtsy and answered, "Liesl."

Agathe preferred to retain her own memories rather than see the movie. It took her sister Maria four years and a ten-hour boat ride to view *The Sound of Music* in New Guinea. Rosmarie saw the film and exclaimed, "Wow! Is this my life? It was much different from what I remember living."

The entire family agreed that the stage and screen characterizations of their father were inaccurate, showing him as stern and autocratic. His kind and loving nature was not emphasized. The Captain's daughter Maria said she eventually became reconciled to the film version, because "It did show that my father had great principles."

The Sound of Music became one of the most popular films ever made. Thirty years after its release, it was estimated that 220,000,000 had seen the movie worldwide. Its financial success was sometimes dubbed "The Sound of Money." "But not for us," Maria claimed. Due to an early sale of the rights to her book, only a tiny fraction of the profits ever reached the family.

In the summer of 1965, the community of Stowe paid tribute to the Trapp Family. During the Stowe Festival of Music, the Trapp Family Singers performed a rare reunion concert on the meadow near the Lodge. Before a large audience, they sang under Father

Right: A rare reunion at the Lodge brought the Trapp Family Singers together again for a concert. From left: Eleonore, Agathe, Maria, Rosmarie, Hedwig, Mother, Johannes, Werner, and Father Wasner. "We haven't sung together for ten years and we were so apprehensive that we could not do it," Maria told the large audience. "And now we are." Two years later the family represented Vermont at Canada's Expo '67, performing again to enthusiastic crowds.

Wasner's direction for the first time in nearly a decade. A White House citation from President Johnson recognized the event:

"It is a pleasure for me to join music lovers everywhere in this richly deserved salute to the Trapp Family. May the music of this Festival echo Vermont's pride in the countless self-less and rewarding accomplishments of the Trapp Family, and may the praise and gratitude which they have so rightfully earned resound through-out our land. Their characteristic devotion to justice and individual dignity, their compassion and dedication to humanity will live forever in the cherished musical legacy which they brought to our shores."

The Sound of Music propelled Maria von Trapp into the life of a famous celebrity. "I had expected to lead a quiet life on a Vermont hill, just dealing with our guests," she observed. Instead, she was recognized wherever she went and was heavily booked as a speaker. She was interviewed on numerous television shows, including those of Julie Andrews, Dinah Shore, and Mike Douglas. She became one of Phil Donahue's favorite guests, and made repeated visits to his talk show.

During the summers in Stowe, thousands of tourists arrived at the Trapp Family Lodge, hoping to meet "The Real Maria from *The Sound of Music*." Maria made regular appearances at the Gift Shop, patiently signed autographs, and posed for photographs. "In times like ours," Maria said, "so filled with 'un-love,' if I can be instrumental in making people

happy, this is a great privilege. If *The Sound of Music* or a book of mine has helped them and changed their lives, then I feel I wouldn't want it any other way. The millions and millions of people who have seen *The Sound of Music* are getting this message: 'The most important thing in life is to find out what is the will of God, and then go and do it.'"

Top Left: *Baroness Maria von Trapp, author and lecturer. She wrote six books: The Story of the Trapp Family Singers; Yesterday, Today and Forever; Around the Year with the Trapp Family; A Family on Wheels; Maria: My Own Story; and When the King Was Carpenter.*

Top Right: *Maria enjoys a stroll at the Trapp Family Lodge. When at home she tried to hike each day. She was also an avid swimmer and horseback rider.*

Above: *Maria was a popular and inspiring lecturer. Some of her speaking engagements took her back to the same stages where she had performed with the family in earlier years.*

One of the great appeals of the The Sound of Music was the breathtaking scenery of the Salzburg region used in the film. As Maria von Trapp said, "The first ten minutes of the film I could see every day at breakfast."

Tourists from all over the world started flocking into Salzburg following the release of the film to see in person the spots they had loved in the movie. Salzburg Panorama Tours was formed to conduct visitors to famous sites in Salzburg and the surrounding countryside. A "Sound of Music Dinner Show" is a daily feature in the Stieglkeller, a large ballroom in the Fortress overlooking Salzburg.

The Trapp Family story is credited with bringing much world wide recognition to Salzburg and Austria. When the Governor of Salzburg visited the Trapp Family Lodge in Stowe, he said that, "Without The Sound of Music, many people would still believe that Austria is a part of Germany."

Right: The Castle Anif was used in an aerial view at the beginning of "The Sound of Music."

The Castle Frohnburg was used to represent the von Trapp home in the movie.

The summer house scene was a great favorite with movie audiences.

Above: The Sound of Music wedding church at Mondsee is a former Benedictine Monastery church.

Top: Historic St. Peter's Cemetery is the oldest cemetery in Austria still in use. This cemetery is also the burial place of Father Franz Wasner. *Above:* Beautiful Mirabelle Gardens, with the Fortress in the background. *Left:* The Rock Riding School in the Festival House was used as the scene of the movie for the Trapp Family's performance of "Edelweiss" and "So Long, Farewell."

Right: The castle of Leopoldskron was used for several sccenes in The Sound of Music. The terrace was where the von Trapp children had lemonade with the Baroness, and Maria and Georg danced on the balcony.

Below: The interior of the church at the small village of Mondsee, near Salzburg, served as the filming site for the "Wedding Scene" of Maria and Georg. The Baroque sculpture and altars are prizes of the region.

Top: "The Sound of Music Dinner Show" takes place at Salzburg's Stieglkeller. Above: "How Do You Solve a Problem like Maria" resounds nightly from a world-wide mix of visitors at the Stieglkeller.

Maria and Johannes at the new Lodge. (Photo: Yankee Images)

CHAPTER 15

Loss and Triumph: The New Lodge

"The success of *The Sound of Music* hasn't changed the family one bit," Rupert remarked in the years following the phenomenal, worldwide fame of the film based on the life of the Trapp Family. Each of the children continued to lead quiet, productive lives, neither desiring nor affecting celebrity status. Werner spoke for his siblings when he said that he discouraged "hero worship or fanship."

When the media located a family member and requested interviews, they were granted with the usual Trapp Family hospitality. The second generation, the twenty-seven cousins, grew up steeped in family heritage, but expected no preferential treatment because of it. As their grandmother explained, "Not one of them has interest in building a choir!" When Kristina, whose father is Johannes, was asked if she sings, she replied, "No better than anyone else."

Through the 1970s, Rupert explained, "The family continued to be close, but not as close as before." They were all saddened by the death of Hedwig in 1972 and gathered in Stowe for her funeral. Hedwig's last teaching post had been high in the Austrian Alps, a location thought to be favorable to her asthmatic condition. Finally, she became too ill to continue teaching. While visiting her aunt in Zell-am-See, she died at the age of fifty-five. She was buried in the family cemetery near the Trapp Family Lodge.

The Lodge became the place of pilgrimage for Trapp Family admirers, and as a resort, it continued to evolve while remaining true to its traditions. While Maria von Trapp remained very much in the limelight at the Lodge, she turned over management to Johannes. "For too many years, I had run the place with my left hand: an emotional mother, with no business sense," she said. Johannes, though trained as a forester, became an innovative manager. His mother sometimes found relinquishment of her role difficult, but she admitted, "I can say, honestly and really truly, that Johannes is doing a great job."

The remains of the Lodge, following the 1980 fire.

For visitors, the excitement of meeting Maria von Trapp was as much a lure as the venerable old Lodge itself. Well into her seventies, Maria continued to pop in the gift shop to sign autographs, and she went from table to table in the dining room, greeting guests. But it was Christmas Eve at the Lodge that she considered the highlight of the year. Maria led the festivities around the Christmas tree including the singing of "Silent Night."

All was in readiness for the holiday at the Lodge on the night of December 20, 1980, when tragedy struck. Deep in the night, fire broke out, and soon the rambling wood-frame lodge was engulfed by flames. A night watchman alerted guests, helping many of them evacuate into the sub-zero temperatures of the winter night. Guests in the Lower Lodge across the street opened their doors to the evacuees, while the sight of the burning building filled the night with horror.

Johannes was alerted from a pay phone. He had the frightening experience of racing to the site and finding no one in evidence, unaware that guests had found shelter in the Lower Lodge. There he found his mother, who escaped with nightgown and slippers.

For Maria, the Lodge fire was a night of sorrows and a narrow escape. Her ninety-three year-old secretary, Ethel Smalley, was asleep in Maria's apartment on the second floor of the Lodge when she awakened to a smoke-filled room. She roused Maria and a guest, Emily Johnson. The three were rescued by another guest, Jerry Lawrence, who led them across the snow-covered balcony and down a slippery ladder.

Stowe firefighters made heroic attempts to save the Lodge, but intense cold and lack of water thwarted efforts. Guests watched with Maria and Johannes as the beloved and historic Lodge was reduced to smoking ruins. At dawn, all that remained were four chimneys, surrounded by a ghostly swirl of steam and smoke. An explanation for the fire was never discovered.

News flashed over the media that the Trapps had lost their Lodge. The evening television news showed Werner as he stood by his stepmother in his steadfast, quiet manner, surveying the site. Rupert arrived to help. Eleonore had watched an orange glow in the sky from her home in Waitsfield, and she called Agathe to report, "It happened . . ." She referred to their father's long-ago dream that the house was afire. Far off in New Guinea, Maria learned the news, but was sure that a new Lodge would emerge from the ashes.

As he observed the smoldering wreck of forty years of family life and lodge business, Johannes told the press, "We will rebuild." But the assertion was as much a challenge as it was a way to console the thousands of concerned friends who wrote, called, and offered their help and prayers.

It was Maria Trapp who was perhaps most devastated by the fire. "I lost just plain everything," she mourned. Gone was a lifetime accumulation of personal papers, family memorabilia, and honoraria. When she emerged from a brief seclusion, she talked to the press and recreated her daily life. She was touched by the massive show of support from friends, both known and unknown. With her characteristic faith, she declared, "It is the will of God that we rebuild."

The rebuilding process was a lengthy one, spanning three years. During that time, limited hospitality was available at the undamaged Lower Lodge and the Austrian tea room down the road. Gradually, a plan for a new Trapp Family Lodge emerged and building began. Along with the enlarged version of the original Lodge, a new concept was added: time-share vacation homes.

The completed Trapp Family Lodge opened its doors to the first visitors in December 1983. The new building was a spectacular combination of modern, comfortable accommodations, with the nostalgic features of the earlier house. The number of rooms was more than doubled, the dining room was spacious, and the kitchen was state-of-the-art. It was a happy day when Johannes gave his mother the first tour and showed her to her new home in Suite 300. "I'm overwhelmed," Maria admitted.

"Our lives are like a bit of theater, and we need a final act," Johannes decided. And so in January 1984, the reopening was celebrated with a memorable Trapp Family event. Old friends from around the world streamed over the snowy hills to the majestic new Lodge. A family reunion of grand magnitude ensued, with Maria arriving from New Guinea, Father Wasner from Salzburg, and children and grandchildren from all over Vermont and beyond.

Sprightly Mary Martin arrived with Mrs. Bob Hope. "It was one of the most beautiful par-

Above: The assembled Trapp Family at the new Lodge opening. Right: Maria and Johannes in front of the new Lodge. Below: Mary Martin joined the family for the opening. Standing: Werner, Eleonore, and Johannes. Seated: Father Wasner, Maria, Rupert, Mother, and Mary.

Over: Horses pull an old fashioned sleigh at the Lodge.

Winter at the Lodge is filled with a variety of activities, from the exciting cross-country ski races to sleigh rides.

Above: This skier enjoys the solitude of the Lodge grounds.

Left: Johannes and wife Lynne head out on the trails.

The Trapp Family
invites you to share
a little of Austria,
a lot of Vermont

Top: The welcoming sign. Above: The rock garden is the oldest of the Lodge gardens.

TEA ROOM
SLEIGH ROAD
AITHER TR.
AYERS TRACK

Winter and summer, guests enjoy the trails

The new Trapp Family Lodge.

Upper right: Pastries have always been famous at the Tea Room.

Above: The Tea Room was formerly home for Werner and his family.

Right: Music is still a tradition: The Trapp Family Concert Meadow.

Below: The comfortable living room is laden with plants.

Bottom: Outdoor activities abound at the Lodge.

ties I have been to," Mary said. "I feel very honored to be a part of Maria's life." Maria, who turned 79 during the festivities, happily surveyed the receptions, dinners, and an Austrian ball. Vacationers again filled the Lodge, and cross-country skiers glided by the new inn. "It's a very grateful time," declared Eleonore.

Although Maria was back at home in the Trapp Family Lodge, her life became a quiet one. The fire had taken its toll. She made occasional forays into public life where she always shone, but these events became rarer. She visited Austria to appear in a British documentary, and was invited to the Reagan White House for dinner, but increasingly she stayed among her beloved mountains. She thought longingly of old Austria. "I would go back," she said, "but I'd stay deep in the country where the old peasants live who haven't changed."

Maria was staying with Emily Johnson when she suffered her last illness. She was 82 years old, and weary. Her old drive and determination had faded. "Mother seemed to flicker away, like a candle," said Werner's wife Erika. "Family members took watch over her, singing and praying," said Werner. "I asked my daughter Elisabeth to read from the fourteenth chapter of John: 'in my father's house are many mansions. . .' Elisabeth, Lorli and Hugh were singing 'To Thee the Holy Ghost, We Now Pray' and just at that moment, Mother opened her eyes with an amazing gaze, and was gone." It was March 28, 1987.

The Trapp Family had lost its strong, creative matriarch. "It's the end of an era," grandson George acknowledged. "She developed everything we have at the Trapp Family Lodge." Mary Martin recalled the song "Climb Ev'ry Mountain" when she paid tribute to Maria von Trapp. "She didn't just climb that mountain," Mary said, "she helped everybody over it!"

When news of Maria's passing spread through Stowe and the world beyond, she was fondly recalled as the heroine of a legendary play and movie, and as the guiding force of one of history's most beloved families. But Maria would possibly be most pleased that her life philosophy was remembered: in seeking God's will, we find peace and happiness.

Left: Maria's beloved Lodge in Autumn.

Below: Maria von Trapp among her favorite things—flowers and mountains.

Bottom: The gravesite of the Captain and Maria.

In Memory of

Maria Augusta von Trapp
1905 – 1987

"The most important thing in life is to find out the Will of God and then do it."

Captain Georg von Trapp 1880-1947

CHAPTER 16

Trapp Traditions Live On

"A group of brothers and sisters is something so precious," declared Maria von Trapp. "They work together and learn from childhood on to watch out for each other and to share." For many years, since the singing group disbanded, the family members were widely scattered, but Trapp Family gatherings increased during the 1980s when six of the children lived in close proximity in Vermont.

After thirty-two years of medical practice in Rhode Island and Massachusetts, Rupert retired to Stowe with his second wife, Jan. They enjoyed travel and music, collaborating on *The Pied Piper's Repertoire*, a manual of recorder music. Jan was a musician, and Rupert was delighted that "nearly every day there is a rehearsal, or music of some kind being performed in our home."

Two of Rupert's sisters also returned to the Stowe area. Maria gave nearly thirty years of her life to mission work in Papua New Guinea before retiring to live near her brothers and sisters. Rosmarie dedicated much of her time to the religious group "Community of the Crucified One" based in Pittsburgh. A branch was formed in Vermont, and Rosmarie became active with the organization there. She also introduced "sing-alongs" to the Trapp Family Lodge, and taught crafts and gave recorder lessons.

The Trapps celebrate a half century in America. Left to right: Rupert, Eleonore, Maria, Johanna and Werner. In front: Johannes and Rosmarie.

A fiftieth anniversary celebration, marking the family's years in America, brought Johanna back to the Lodge. With her husband Ernst, she had lived for many years near Vienna, raising their seven children. During their respective retirement years, the brothers and sisters visited back and forth, and reminisced over the multitude of experiences they shared.

Rupert, the senior member of the family, died in 1992 at the age of eighty. He had lived perhaps the most independent life of his siblings, leaving the singing group early to give his life to medicine. But he was dedicated to tradition and especially hoped that the Trapp Family's musical heritage would endure.

The man who was so much a part of the music, Franz Wasner, died a few months after Rupert. He had spent seven years as a missionary in the Fiji Islands, and then served as rector of "Anima," the German-speaking House of Studies in Rome. In 1982 Father Wasner retired to Salzburg as a canon of the Cathedral. He made trips to America, and the Trapps visited him when they came to Austria. Composing and playing music continued to fill Father Wasner's days until his death at the age of eighty-six.

Dr. Rupert von Trapp

145

Johanna in 1993.

Two years later, in 1994, Johanna died in Vienna from the aftereffects of a stroke. She had been prolific in her pursuit of arts and crafts, and was creative in many mediums. A year before her death, an exhibit was held in Salzburg featuring the work of Johanna, Maria, and Agathe. Johanna attended, and had frequently traveled to visit her children and grandchildren scattered around the world.

❖⟹◁❖

Despite the major recognition that came to Captain von Trapp's family, his children never felt satisfied that their father received his just tribute. He had heroically served his country and his family, and finally—fifty years after his death—his deeds were celebrated.

An overwhelming vote of cadets at the Theresianum, the Austrian equivalent of West Point, named Georg von Trapp as hero for the graduating class of 1997. A meeting with daughter Maria von Trapp in Vienna result-

Right: Werner's daughter Elizabeth is the only member of the second generation who has pursued music professionally. She performs in a variety of settings, including the Trapp Family Lodge, and has recorded music she has written and arranged.

ed in her invitation to the class to "Come and see us in Stowe, Vermont." Following clearance from the United States Government and permission from their own defense minister, nearly one hundred Austrians arrived at the Trapp Family Lodge on July 12, 1997 for events both joyous and solemn.

The visit had political significance. Austrian Consul General Dr. Walter Greinert acknowledged that the cadets' tribute recognized the correct decision of the Captain in 1938 to lead his family out of Nazi-occupied Austria. Cadet Rainer Winter likened the Captain's life to the Academy's motto: "Good Officers and Righteous Men." It was also remembered that Georg von Trapp served his homeland after World War II by founding the Trapp Family Austrian Relief.

While the cadets explored the acres that their hero had called his American home, the Captain's descendants assembled. Each of the living children was present: Agathe, Maria, Werner, Rosmarie, Eleonore, and Johannes. There were grandchildren and great grandchildren by the dozens.

A Sunday field mass was held for the Captain, in view of his burial site in the Lodge garden. Family and friends sang Schubert's "German Mass," accompanied by the Mozart Festival Orchestra. Once more the Captain's children stood in a row to sing, with a long line of cadets nearby and the Green Mountains all around.

"His was a remarkable life to inspire all of us," said Cadet Winter, as his comrades placed a commemorative wreath on the Captain's grave. "He cared for his men, and they rewarded him with their trust. Georg von Trapp's decision to leave the country rather than serve in the armed forces of Adolf Hitler was a difficult one. We think he made the right choice."

From his life at sea to his life at home, Captain Georg von Trapp lived nobly. He practiced the qualities of faith, honor, duty, and love all his days. And he taught his children those life principles, in Austria and America, during good times and bad. His values became the Trapp Family traditions, and "by their deeds they are known."

Above: Maria greets her grand-nieces, Sofia and Amanda von Trapp, who came to honor their great grandfather.

Overleaf: The Trapp Family Lodge in Stowe is still a magnet for the family. Here they gathered in July 1997 with Austrian cadets who came to honor Captain von Trapp.

A HERO HONORED

Maria, Eleonore, Werner, Rosmarie and Agathe sing the Schubert "German Mass."

The honor for Captain von Trapp brought family members and old friends together for an historic reunion.

Left: Maria lights the vigil lamp on her father's grave.

Consul general of Austria, Walter Greinert, remarked of the ceremonies at the Trapp Family Lodge:

"On the one side, I am here to express our appreciation of the fact that the von Trapp family always stood for patriotism and righteousness. On the other side, I am here as a representative of a new Austria in a new Europe. We are a new generation now, putting behind us some of the troubles of the past."

Above: A wreath is placed in honor of Baron Georg von Trapp.

Right: A salute at the gravesite.

Top row: Rosmarie, Agathe and Maria, Eleonore. Bottom row: Werner, Agathe, and Johannes.

CHAPTER 17

The Trapp Family Today

AGATHE

Agathe (left), the family's gifted artist, assisted in the operation of Sacred Heart kindergarten until her retirement in 1993. Under her direction, a boy's choir sang requiems and High Masses in Gregorian chant. She continues to paint enthusiastically, and some of her work permanently adorns the walls of the Trapp Family Lodge. Also a skilled historian, Agathe researched the Trapp family genealogy, and wrote a book of her memories of life in Austria and the years with the Trapp Family Singers. She lives in Maryland.

Agathe von Trapp

MARIA

Maria's return to Vermont from Papua New Guinea was welcomed by family and friends. She remains a tireless world traveler, enthusiastically pursuing composing and making music with her accordion. Maria's genuine interest in people and her jolly, ready laughter make her a happy addition to life and activities at the Trapp Family Lodge. She has been frequently called upon for speaking engagements and television appearances on programs like "Good Morning America" and the "Oprah Winfrey Show."

Maria von Trapp

WERNER

"There is never a dull moment in my life, and not enough time to do all the things I could or would do," Werner said of the years since his retirement from farming in 1979. He lives in a quiet glen with his wife Erika, busy with gardening and hobbies. He spins wool from his sheep on an antique wheel found by sister Hedwig, and weaves rugs on his workshop loom. Several of his six children and their families live nearby. Music is still important to Werner, and his favorite composer is Mozart. *"He is the one who always lifts me up,"* Werner explains. *"He writes in such a way that always brings joy to my soul."*

The Trapp family's interest in agriculture is carried on by Werner's son Martin on the family farm near Waitsfield.

Tobias, one of Werner's sons, is involved in nursery work. His Von Trapp Nursery provides seasonal beauty for the homes of the Waitsfield-Stowe area.

ROSMARIE

Rosmarie pursued many interests following her years of singing with the family. She found great fulfillment in her involvement with the "Community of the Crucified One," which has a branch in a beautiful country setting between Stowe and Waitsfield. She continues to be very musical, and shares her joy of group singing and recorder playing with guests at the Trapp Family Lodge.

Rosmarie Trapp

"Music is like food; we need it regularly," declares Maria von Trapp. "There is a spiritual power in music; if the world sang together, there could be no war."

Rosmarie agrees with her sister, and believes in the healing power of music for everyone. Rosmarie's "sing-a-longs" at the Trapp Family Lodge are regular events for guests.

Together with Christina Tourin, Maria and Rosmarie collaborated on the recording "Folk Harp Music of Austria" in 1994. Christina has often performed on her harp in the Lodge dining room; the recording included several of Maria's original compositions.

Maria, at left, on accordion, and Rosmarie on recorder.

ELEONORE

Eleonore, known to family and friends as "Lorli," was described by Rupert as "the most hospitable person I know." She and her husband Hugh Campbell raised seven daughters. In 1975 they moved to Vermont and settled on a portion of Werner's farmland. There Lorli gardens extensively and welcomes a continuous stream of family and friends. At holiday time, the Campbells decorate a sixteen-foot Christmas tree in the old way—with wax candles.

Lorli Campbell

Lorli and husband Hugh enjoy visits of children and grandchildren, and their home is often full of visitors. Here they pose with daughter Martina Price and her daughters Emily and Becky.

Of the family history, Eleonore says, "I think people have a need for hope. The family story showed that trust in God is honored."

"People always ask, 'Which one are you?' We expect questions, and I don't mind answering them. I think it's natural that people are curious."

JOHANNES

Johannes has spent most of his career at the Trapp Family Lodge, where many of his innovations have added to the guests' enjoyment. Johannes and his wife Lynne, a native of Minnesota, were married in the hillside stone chapel behind the Trapp Family Lodge. They have spent their married life near the Lodge, raising two children, Kristina and Sam. The children experienced growing up in close proximity with their grandmother Maria, on the land their father has known since his boyhood.

"Every member of my family discovered something wonderful in these mountains to enrich their lives," says Johannes von Trapp. "We invite you to come share in the grandeur of this place, once our family home, and now the Trapp Family Lodge."

Right: Johannes, his son Sam, and the Trapp Family Tree, which is prominently displayed in the Lodge.

Chronology

1880	Georg von Trapp born
1890	Agathe Whitehead born
1905	Maria Augusta Kutschera born
	Franz Wasner born
1911	January: Marriage of Georg von Trapp and Agathe Whitehead
	November: Rupert born
1913	Agathe born
1914-1918	World War I
1914	Maria born
1915	Werner born
1917	Hedwig born
1919	Johanna born
1921	Martina born
1922	Agathe Whitehead von Trapp dies
1925	Trapp family moves to Salzburg
1926	Maria Kutschera a novice at Nonnberg Abbey
1927	Maria a governess at Trapp home; marriage of Georg and Maria
1929	Rosmarie born
1931	Eleonore born
1935	Formation of Trapp Family Choir

The Captain and Agathe

Maria, Hedwig, Johanna and Martina pose as sailors as they commorate their father's naval feats.

On Tour

1943

1946

Australia, 1955

1936-1937	Early concert tours of Trapp Family Choir
1938	Austria annexed by Germany; Trapp Family leaves Salzburg; first American tour
1939	Johannes born; tours of Europe and United States
1940	Columbia Concerts first manages Trapp Family Singers
1941	Trapp Family buys Stowe, Vermont farm
1943	Rupert and Werner enter U.S. Army
1944	First season of Trapp Family Music Camp
1945	End of World War II; safe return of Rupert and Werner
1947	Establishment of Trapp Family Austrian Relief Death of Georg von Trapp
1948	Family members become American citizens; Werner married; Johanna married
1949	*The Story of the Trapp Family Singers* published; marriage of Martina
1950	Trapp Family Singers tour South America and Europe
1951	Death of Martina
1952	Hawaiian concert tour
1953	Father Franz Wasner elevated to rank of Monsignor
1954	Eleonore married

The Bay Window, 1953

In the Green Mountains

1955	Australia-New Zealand concert tour
1956	Final concert performances; Music Camp disbands
	German film *Die Trapp Familie* appears
1959	*The Sound of Music* debuts on Broadway
1965	*The Sound of Music* released as a movie
1967	Maria von Trapp honored by Austria with "Honorary Cross, First Class"
1969	Johannes married; cross-country skiing is pioneered at Trapp Family Lodge
1972	Death of Hedwig
1980	Trapp Family Lodge destroyed by fire
1983	Reopening of Trapp Family Lodge
1987	Death of Maria Augusta von Trapp
1992	Death of Rupert; death of Franz Wasner
1993	Trapp Family honored by Governor of Salzburg
1994	Death of Johanna
1997	Georg von Trapp honored by Austrian military students
1998	The Sound of Music returns to Broadway
	The Trapp Family are awarded "The Golden Decoration of Honor" of the State of Salzburg

Australia, 1955

Hawaii, 1952

NY, 1998. The Trapps celebrate with the 7 children actors who portrayed them in the 1965 "The Sound of Music" movie at Austrian awards ceremony.

Discography

The Trapp Family began recording their unique repertoire within two months of their arrival in America. On December 16, 1938, the group first assembled in RCA Victor's New York studio, recording for posterity the sound of the original choir. Their last recordings were made in 1956. The Trapp Family Singers' career in recording spanned every medium in recorded sound, from 78 rpm records, long-play albums, cassette reissues, and finally compilations of their work on state-of-the-art compact discs. They have been called by conductor Robert Shaw "the greatest choral group in the history of recorded sound."

RCA VICTOR

Innsbruck, ich muss dich lassen; Landsknechständchen (Soldier's Serenade); Es ist ein Ros Entsprungen (Lo, How a Rose e're Blooming); Frienslieb du hast mich gefangen (My Love, You Have Bewitched Me); Tanzen und Springen (Dancing and Skipping) (Recorded 12/16/38)

Zu Bethlehem Geboren (In Bethlehem Born); Wohlauf ihr lieben Gäste (Now Then, Dear Guests); Die Martinsgans (St. Martin's Goose); Audite Nova; Ein Hennlein Weiss (A Little White Hen); Mein eingis A (My Own A); Il Bianco e dolce Cigno (The Sweet White Swan) (Recorded 12/17/38)

Wach Auf, Wach Auf (Awake, Awake); Der Mond is Aufgegangen (The Moon Has Risen); Come, Heavy Sleep; Andreas Hofer's Abschied von Leben (Andreas Hofer's Farewell to Life); In einem kuhlen Grunde (In a Cool Dale); Bist einmel kommen (Once thou camest to Redeem Us) (Recorded 12/21/38)

Es Wird scho glei dumpa (It's Getting Dark); Der Spate Abend (Late One Evening); Lavanthal, Lavanthal (Valley of Lavant); Die Aüglein voll Wasser; Maria durch ein Dornwald ging (In the Thorny Woods); Schoenster Herr Jesu (Recorded 12/22/38)

The

TRAPP FAMILY

Records Exclusively for

VICTOR RED SEAL RECORDS

O Haupt Voll Blut und Wunden (Oh Head All Scarred and Bleeding); Wie Schön Leuchtet der Morgenstern; Jesu Meine Freude (An all-Bach recording session on 10/16/39)

Von Himmel Hoch (From Heaven High); Nun Danket Alle Gott; Lobt Gott ihr Christen Allzugleich; Wer Nur den Lieben Gott Lässt Walten (More Bach, recorded 10/17/39)

Wachet Auf Ruft uns Die Stimme; Lobe Den Herren; Dir, Dir Jehova; Netherland Dances for Recorders: Rondo, Pavane, Intrade, Sarabande, Gigue (Recorded 10/18/39)

Guten Abend, Gut Nacht; Waldesnacht; In Stiller Nacht; Lullabye (an all-Brahms session recorded 2/5/40)

Selections from Palestrina's Missa Brevis, including: Kyrie, Gloria, Agnus Dei (recorded on 2/20/40)

Stille Nacht (Silent Night); Selections from Missa Brevis, including: Gloria, Part 2, Credo, Part 1, Credo, Conclusion, Sanctus, Benedictus; Away in a Manger; Eriskay Love Lilt; Kindersegen (Child's Blessing) (Recorded 2/21/40)

Midwinter; God Rest You Merry, Gentlemen; Cradle Song; In Dulce Jubilo (Recorded at The Academy of Music, Philadelphia, on 6/26/41)

(Note: The above selections were issued as singles and compiled into albums of 78 rpm records under such collection titles as Folk Songs of Central Europe and Missa Brevis - Bach Chorales Album. In 1954, five Christmas songs were reissued in a 45 rpm extended-play recording entitled The Trapp Family: Christmas Songs.)

CONCERT HALL SERIES

The long-forgotten Concert Hall Society label, which recorded classical artists soon after long-play albums were introduced, engaged the Trapp Family Singers for two releases. They were most likely recorded in late 1950 or early in 1951, before the death of Martina in February of that year. *At Home With the Trapp Family Singers* simulates a concert, with the appropriate groups of music: sacred, instrumental, madrigals, Austrian folk music, and folk songs from several countries. Selections include: Meerstern, ich Dich grüsse; The Children's Blessing; Jesu, Joy of Man's Desiring; Fahren wir froh im Nachen; Ein Hennlein Weiss; The Soldier's Serenade; The Silver Swan; Pastorale (Instrumental); Siliciana and Allegro (Instrumental); Austrian Folk Dance (Instrumental); Und Wan I Geh; Vom Zillertal Aussa; Echo Yodel; Old Black Joe; Riquiran; Evening Prayer from Hänsel and Gretel. (This album was rereleased circa 1960 as *Sing Along With the Trapp Family* on the Baronet label of New York City.)

Sacred Music Around the Church Year musically recorded the liturgical year from Advent through Pentecost. The first selections are from Father Wasner's Mass for A Cappella Choir: Sanctus and Benedictus. Fifteen other selections include: Maria durch ein Dornwald ging; Psallite Unigenito; Jesu Redemptor Omnium; Resonet in Laudibus; O Bone Jesu; Jesu, Salvator Mundi; O Salutaris Hostia; Wer Leucht' uns denn bei der finsteren Nacht?; Crux Fidelis; Tenebrae Factae Sunt; Surrexit Pastor Bonus; Regina Coeli, Laetare; To Thee the Holy Ghost, We Now Pray; O Maria Diana Stella; Salve Regina.

The Higbee Company

and RCA Victor

present . . .

The Trapp Family Choir
on long playing albums

each 5.95

DECCA RECORDS

The Decca Record Company recorded five LP albums with the Trapp Family Singers on its Gold Label series from 1951-1956. These have become the most familiar and definitive recordings of the group.

Christmas With the Trapp Family Singers appeared in 1951 at a release price of $5.85. The recording approximated the famous Town Hall holiday concerts. Selections included: Es ist ein Ros entsprungen; Hirten, wachet auf!; Zu Bethlehem Gebohren; Deck the Hall; A la Nanita Nana; Il est né, le divin infant; La canzone di Natale; Es hat sich heut' eröffnet; Jesus, Jesus, Rest your Head; Shepherds come a-running; Lobt-Gott, ihr Christen alle gleich; Es wird scho glei dumpa; Nu är det Jul igen; Ihr Kinderlein, kommet; Der Scheibendudler; Carol of the Drum; Deine Wangelen; Stille Nacht. (This is no doubt the most widely released recording of the Trapp Family Singers. It was rereleased in the 1980s by MCA Records, both in LP and cassette tape versions, and in the 1990s by the Laserlight Company.)

Christmas With the Trapp Family Singers, Volume 2 was recorded in 1953, including Charlene and Harold Peterson as singers and instrumentalists. Contents were: Angelus Ad Pastores In Nativitate Domini; Puer Natus Est Nobis; Beata Viscera; Pastorale (Recorders); Quem Pastores Laudavere; Senex Puerum Portabat; Ave Maria; I Sing of a Maiden; El Rorro; The Christmas Nightingale; Bring Your Torches, Jeanette, Isabella; Angels We Have Heard on High; Bethlehem; The Christmas Rose; Quittez, Pasteurs; Pastores a Belen; From Heaven High.